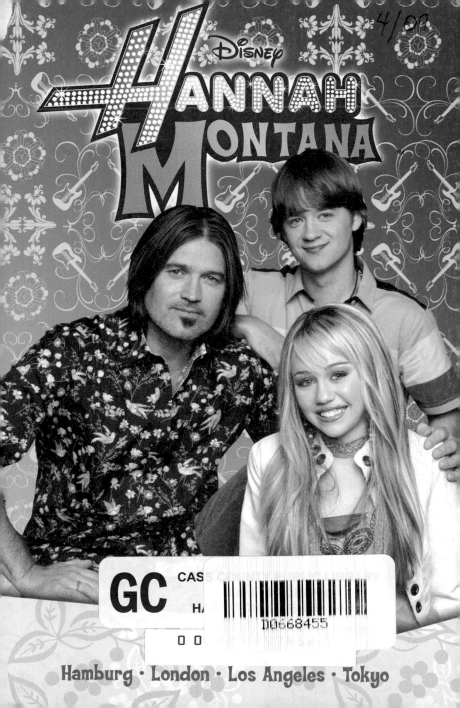

4/99

**Disney**

# HANNAH MONTANA

Hamburg · London · Los Angeles · Tokyo

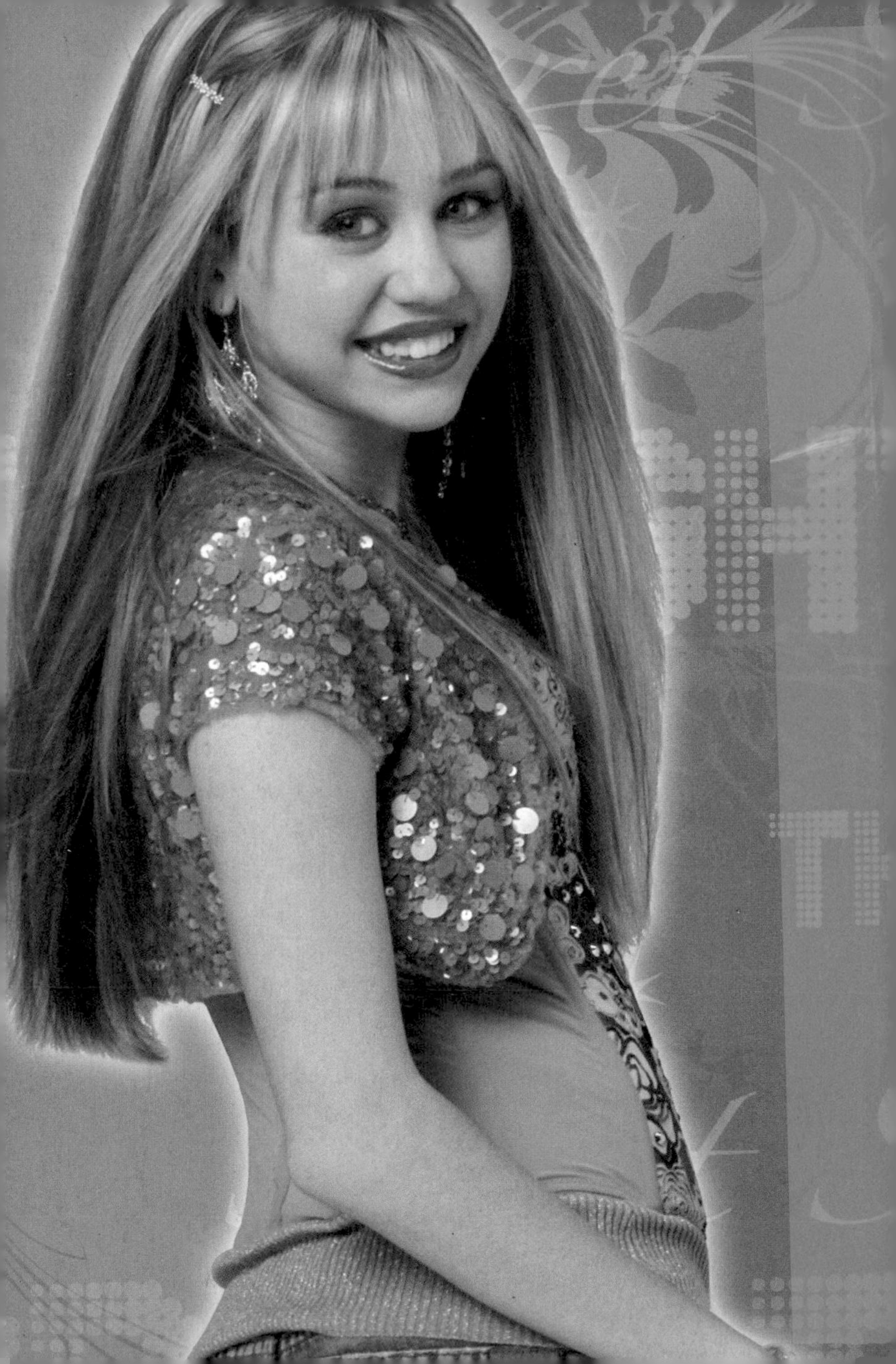

DISNEP

HANNAH MONTANA™

Based on the series created by Michael Poryes and Rich Correll & Barry O'Brien

# CARS AND SUPERSTARS

## "New Kid in School"
Written By Todd J. Greenwald

## "More than a Zombie to Me"
Written By Steven Peterman

Editor - Julie Taylor
Contributing Editors - Marion Brown and Elizabeth Hurchalla
Graphic Designer and Letterer - Anna Kernbaum
Cover Designer - Lindsay Seligman
Graphic Artist - Tomás Montalvo-Lagos

Production Manager - Elisabeth Brizzi
Creative Director - Anne Marie Horne
Editor in Chief - Rob Tokar
Publisher - Mike Kiley
President & C.O.O. - John Parker
C.E.O. & Chief Creative Officer - Stuart Levy

E-mail: info@TOKYOPOP.com
Come visit us online at www.TOKYOPOP.com

A 🐢 TOKYOPOP® Cine-Manga® Book
TOKYOPOP Inc.
5900 Wilshire Blvd., Suite 2000
Los Angeles, CA 90036

Hannah Montana Volume 4
© 2007 Disney

ISBN: 978-1-4278-0786-1

First TOKYOPOP® printing: November 2007

10  9  8  7  6  5  4  3  2

Printed in the USA

# CARS AND SUPERSTARS

CONTENTS

"New Kid in School"................................8
"More than a Zombie to Me"...................48

# WHO'S WHO

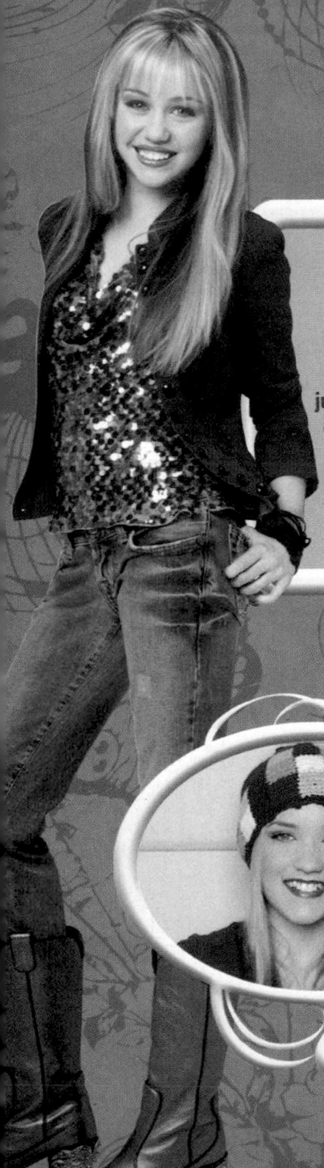

## HANNAH MONTANA/ MILEY STEWART

She's the girl next door who just so happens to moonlight as a world-famous pop sensation. But underneath the glamour of a superstar, Miley Stewart is a regular girl who gets into all kinds of sticky situations.

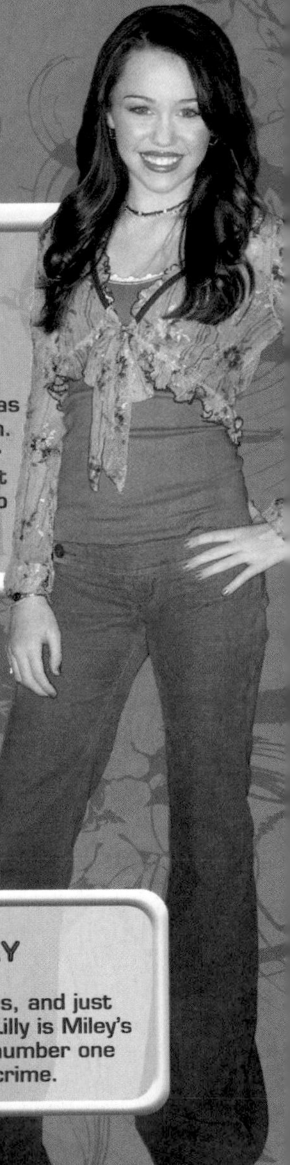

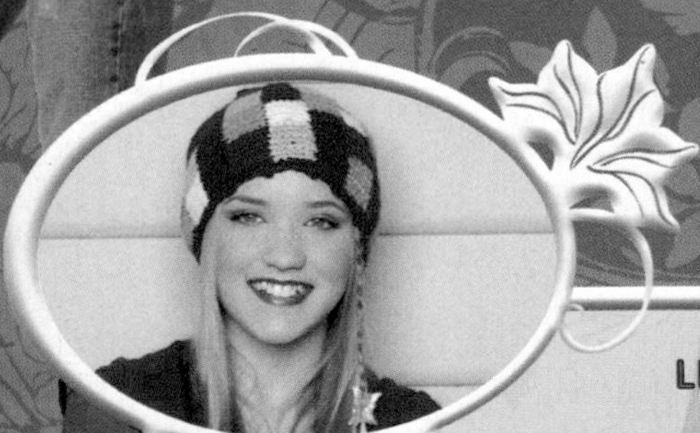

## LILLY

Fun, spontaneous, and just a little bit wacky, Lilly is Miley's best friend and number one partner in crime.

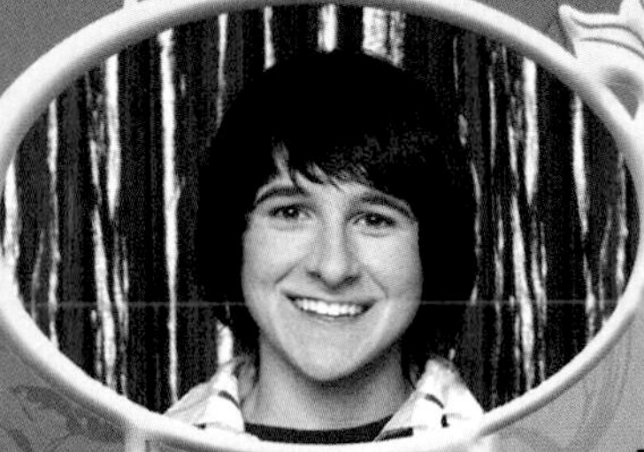

## OLIVER

A super-cool goofball, Oliver is a good friend of both Miley and Lilly.

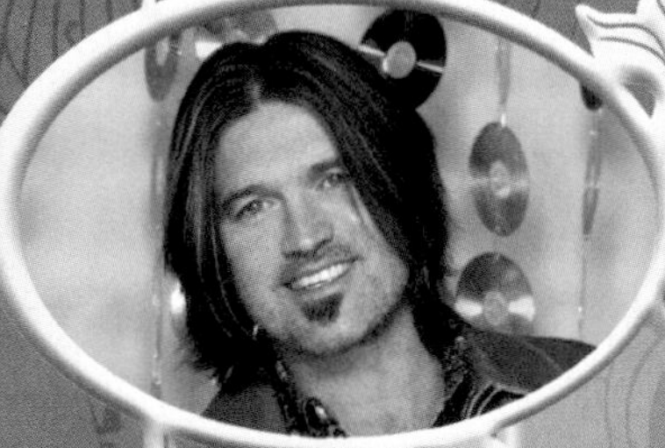

## ROBBY

Miley's dad knows enough about showbiz to keep his little girl, the pop star, rock solid.

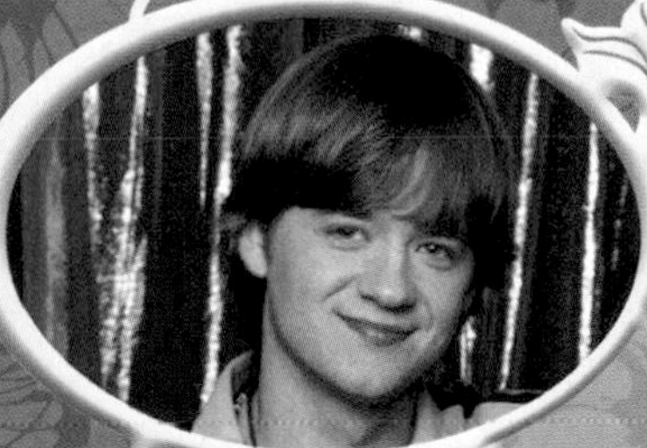

## JACKSON

More silly than slick, Miley's brother Jackson definitely has his own way of doing things.

# NEW KID IN SCHOOL

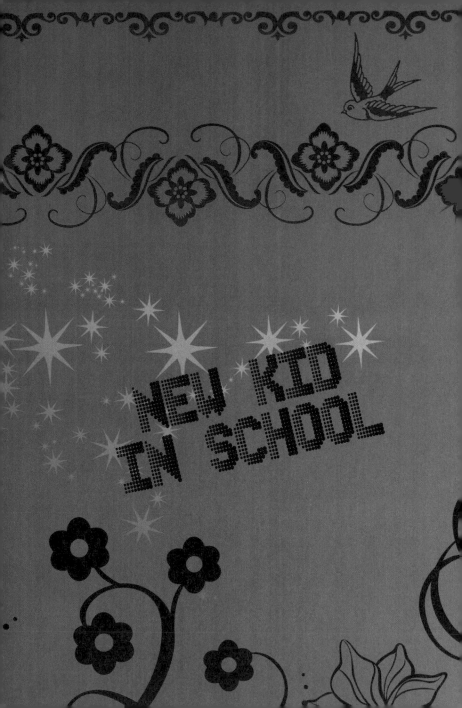

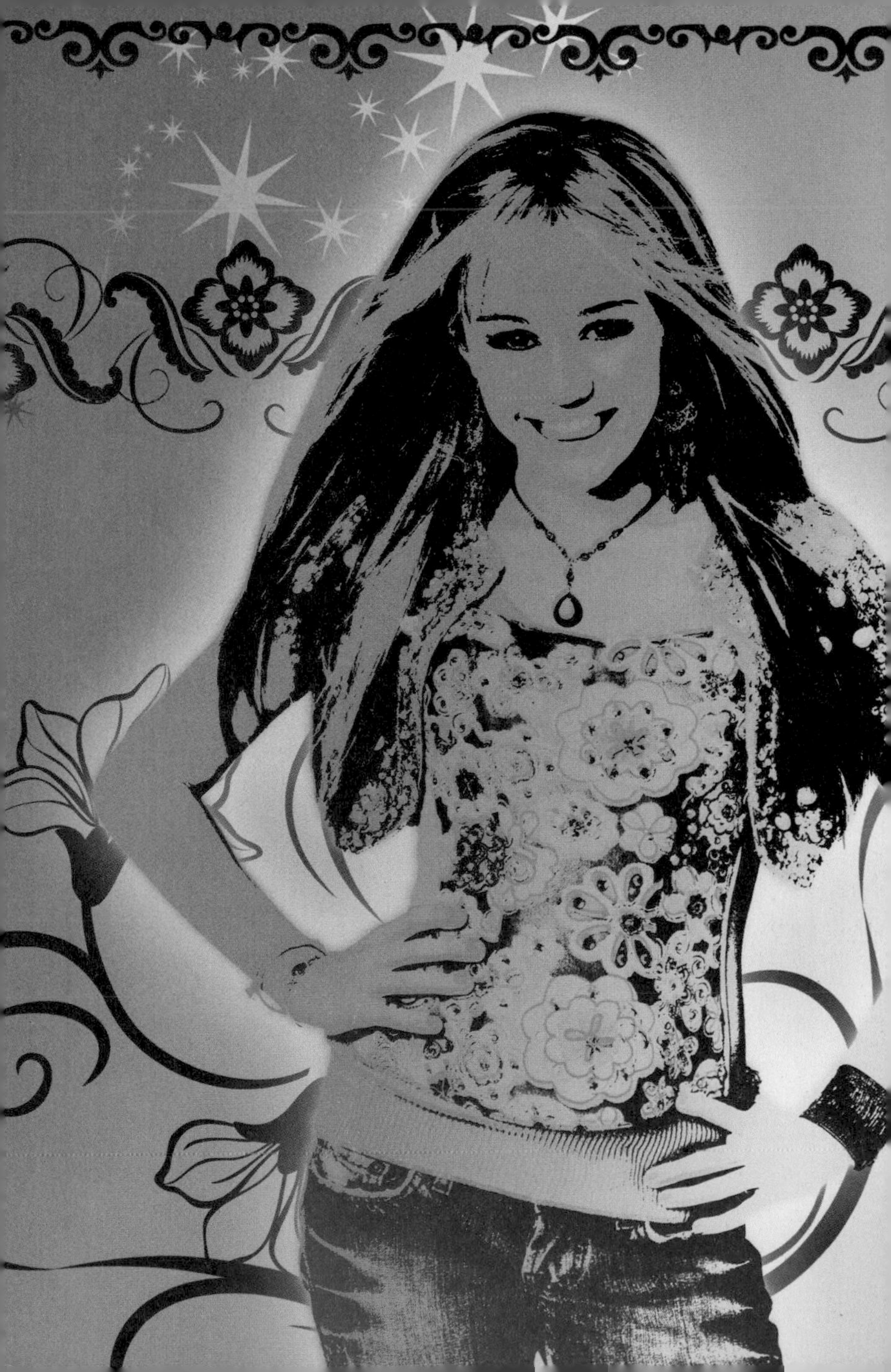

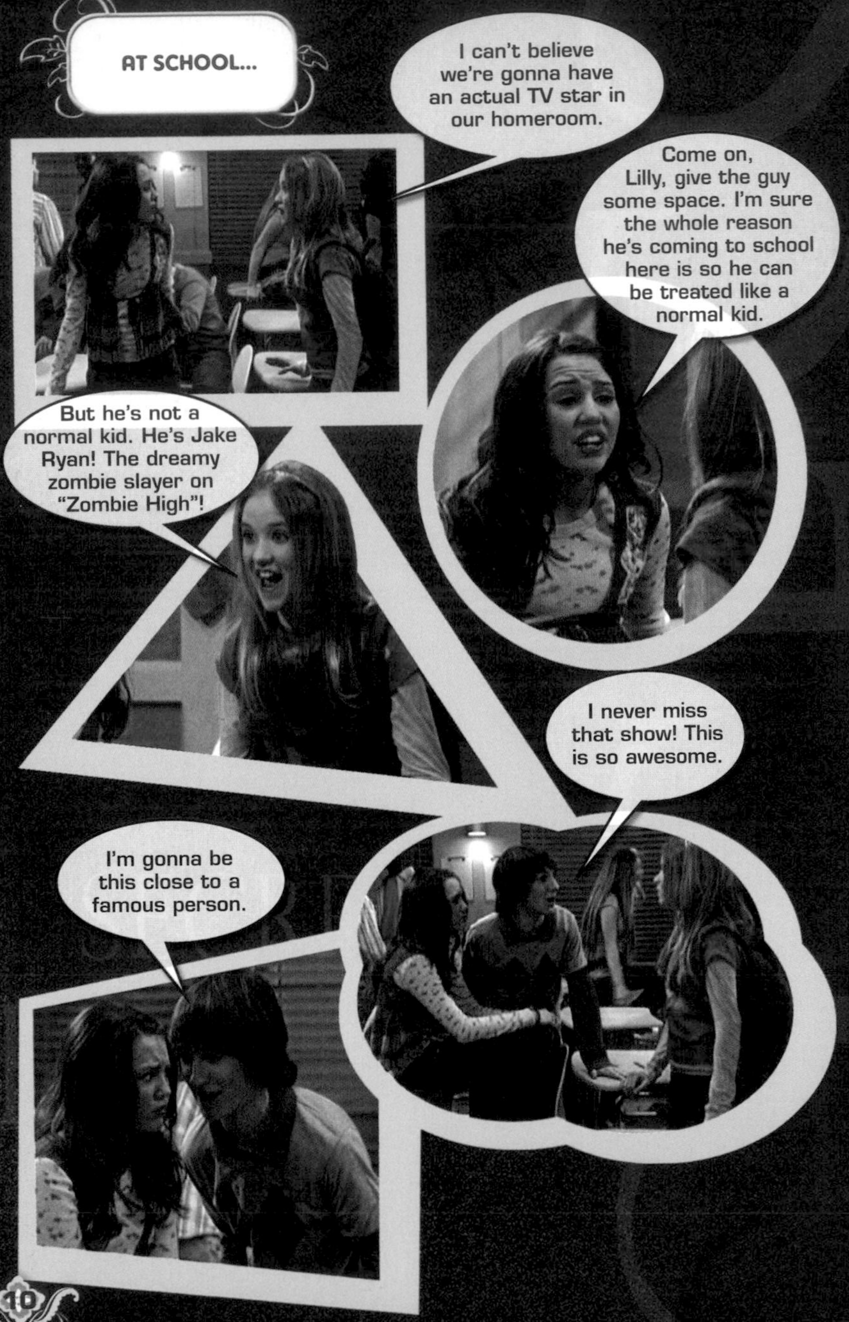
AT SCHOOL...
I can't believe we're gonna have an actual TV star in our homeroom.
Come on, Lilly, give the guy some space. I'm sure the whole reason he's coming to school here is so he can be treated like a normal kid.
But he's not a normal kid. He's Jake Ryan! The dreamy zombie slayer on "Zombie High"!
I'm gonna be this close to a famous person.
I never miss that show! This is so awesome.

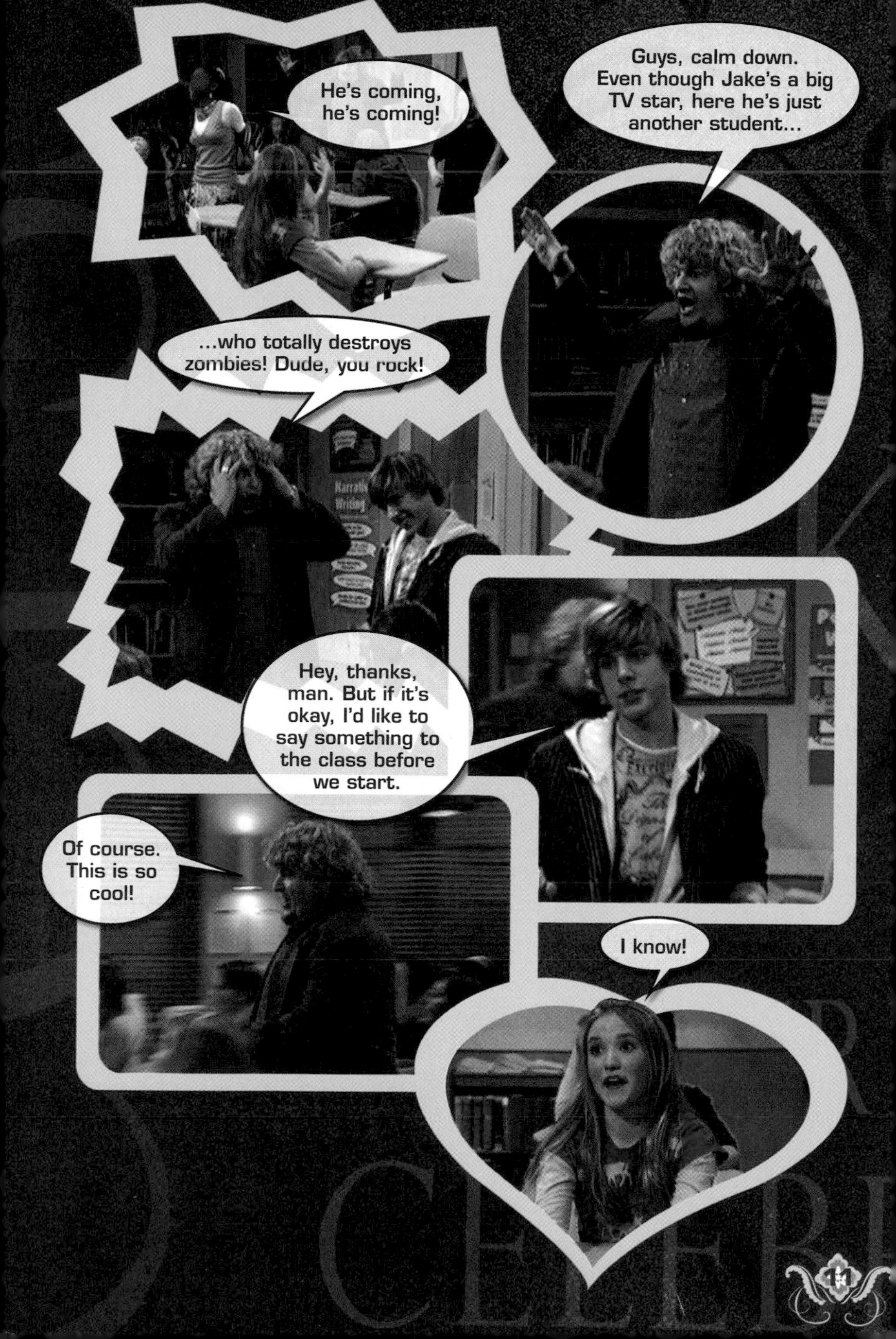
He's coming, he's coming!
Guys, calm down. Even though Jake's a big TV star, here he's just another student...
...who totally destroys zombies! Dude, you rock!
Hey, thanks, man. But if it's okay, I'd like to say something to the class before we start.
Of course. This is so cool!
I know!

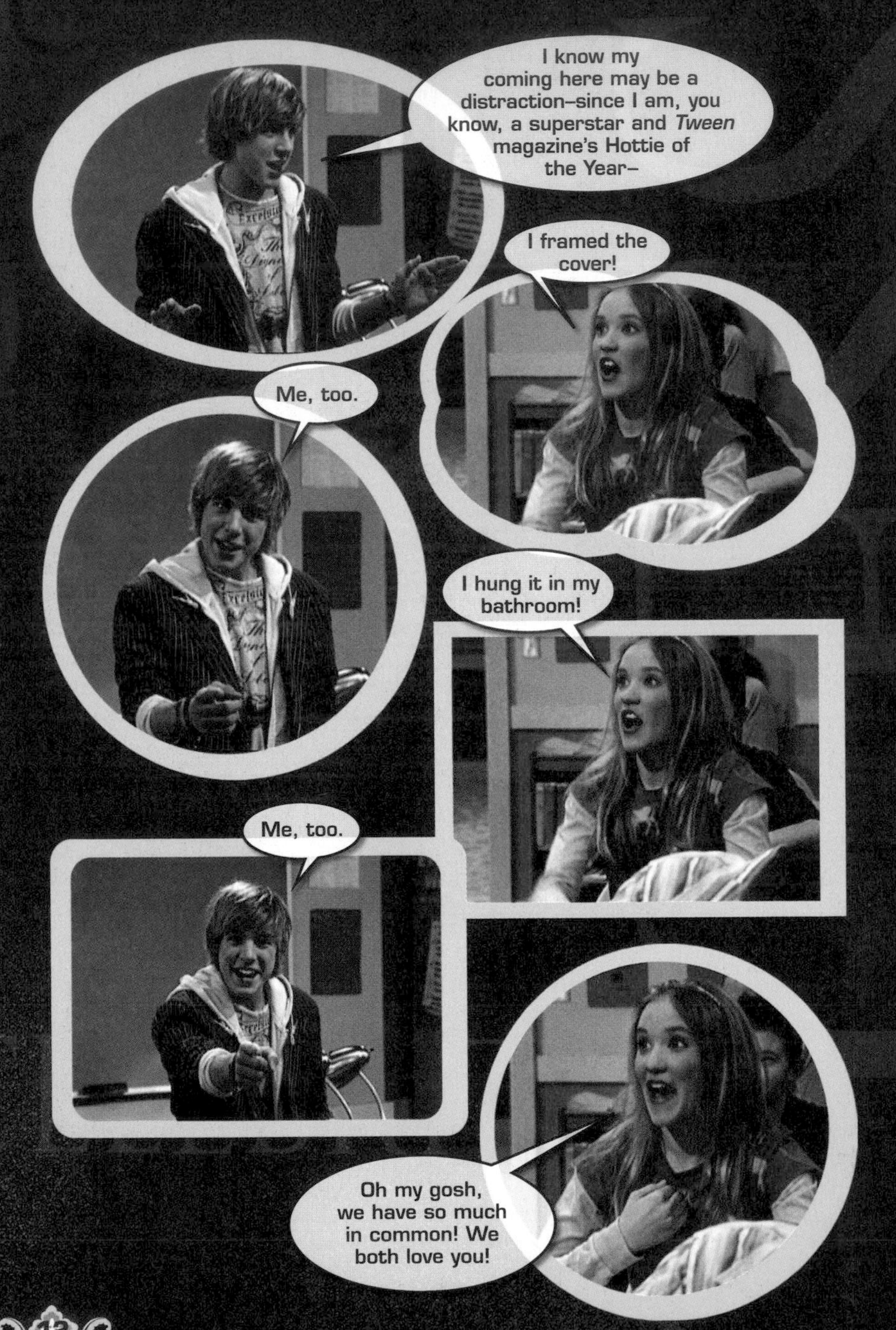
I know my coming here may be a distraction–since I am, you know, a superstar and *Tween* magazine's Hottie of the Year–
I framed the cover!
Me, too.
I hung it in my bathroom!
Me, too.
Oh my gosh, we have so much in common! We both love you!

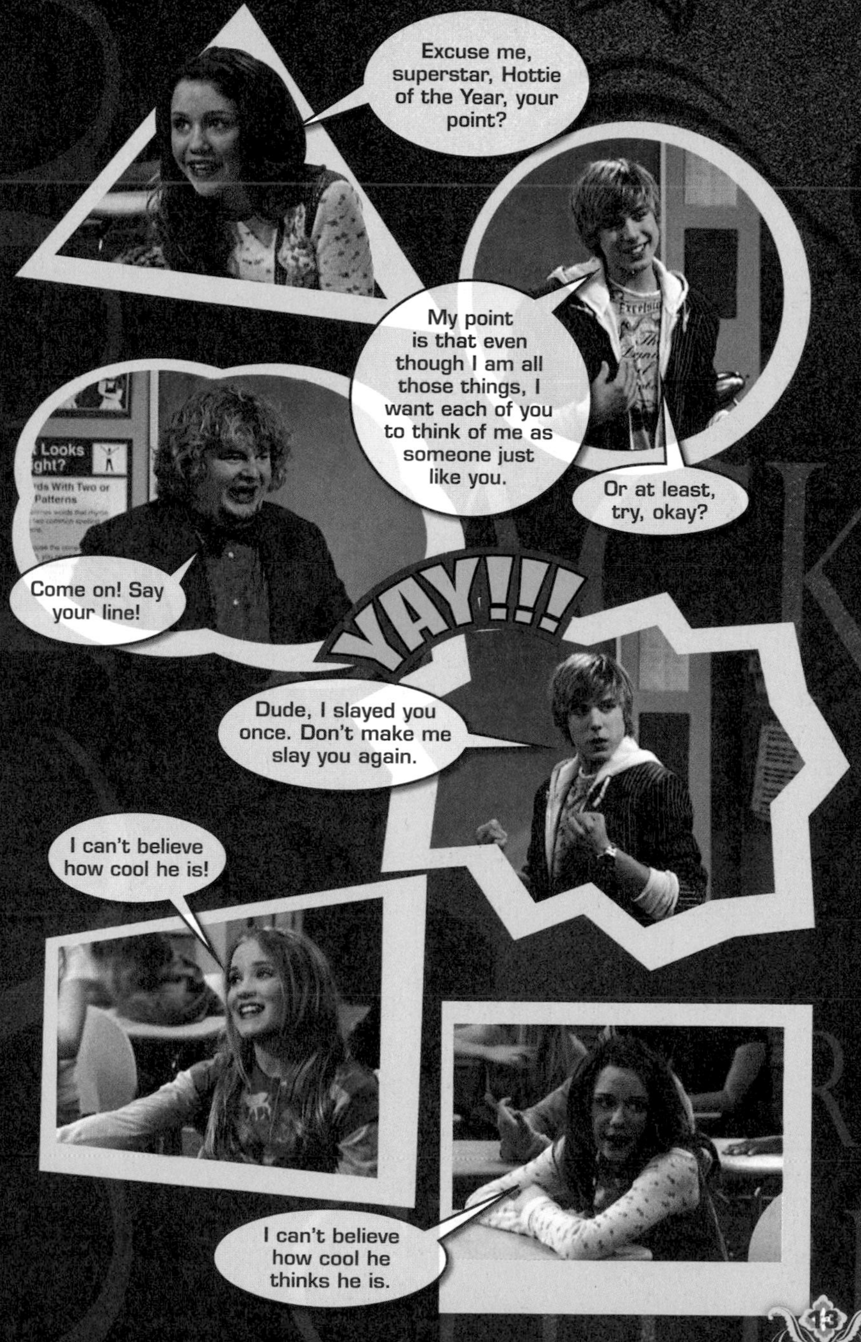

Excuse me, superstar, Hottie of the Year, your point?
My point is that even though I am all those things, I want each of you to think of me as someone just like you.
Or at least, try, okay?
Come on! Say your line!
YAY!!!
Dude, I slayed you once. Don't make me slay you again.
I can't believe how cool he is!
I can't believe how cool he thinks he is.

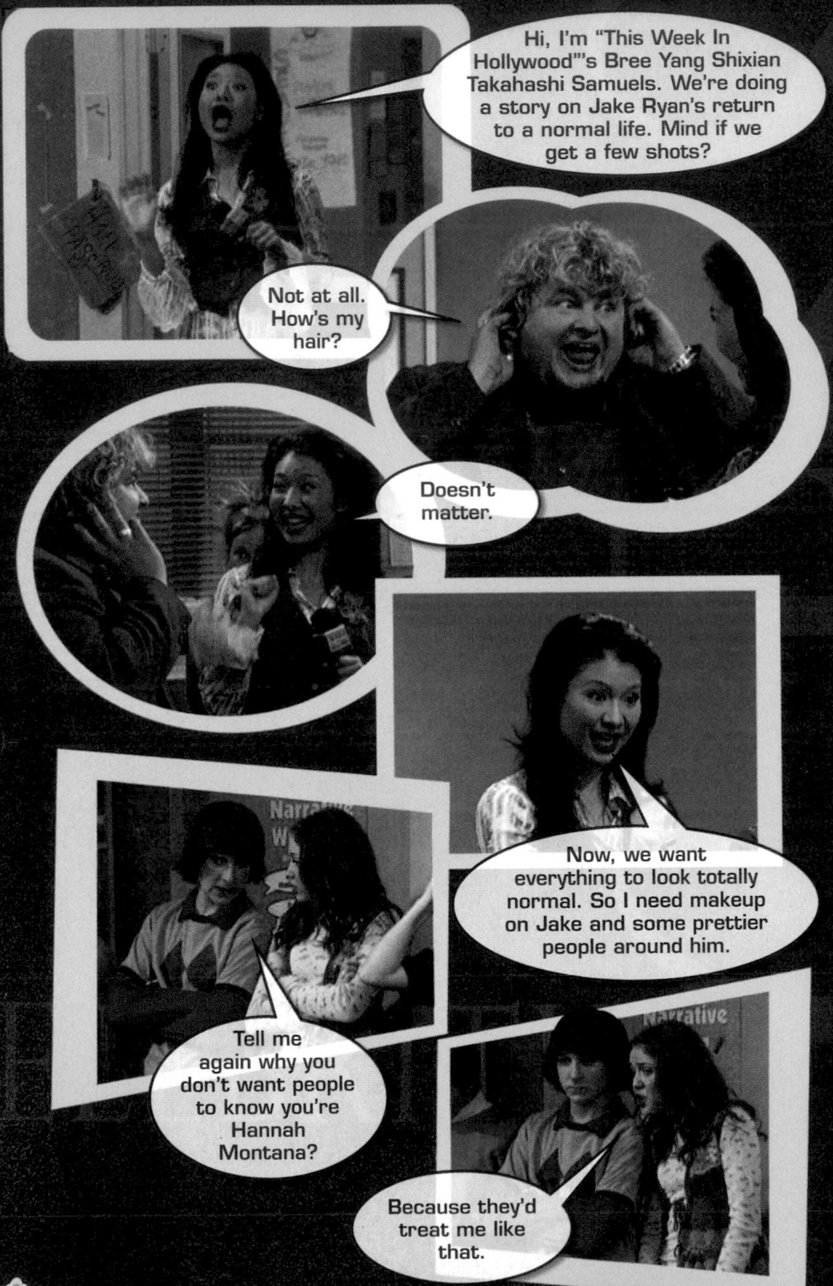
Hi, I'm "This Week In Hollywood"'s Bree Yang Shixian Takahashi Samuels. We're doing a story on Jake Ryan's return to a normal life. Mind if we get a few shots?
Not at all. How's my hair?
Doesn't matter.
Now, we want everything to look totally normal. So I need makeup on Jake and some prettier people around him.
Tell me again why you don't want people to know you're Hannah Montana?
Because they'd treat me like that.

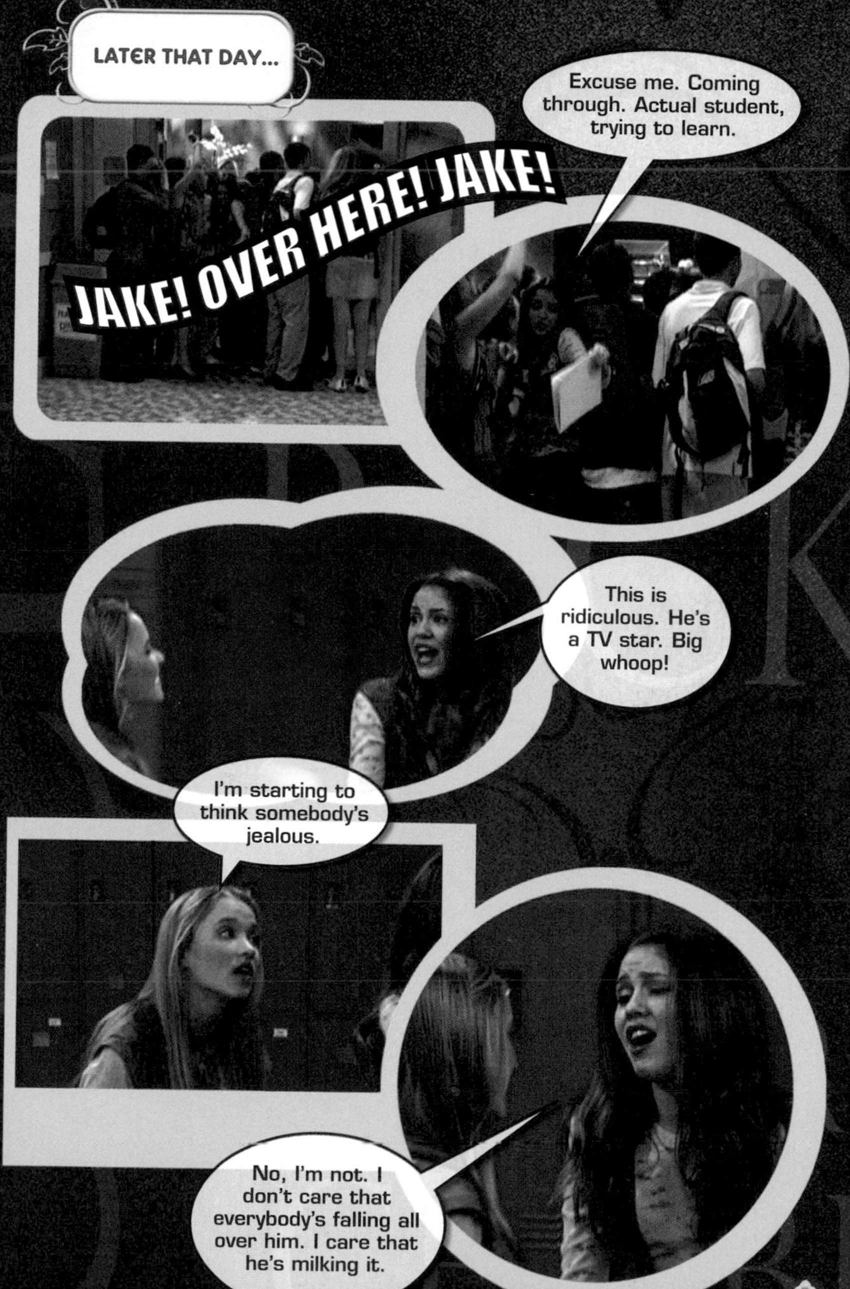
LATER THAT DAY...
JAKE! OVER HERE! JAKE!
Excuse me. Coming through. Actual student, trying to learn.
This is ridiculous. He's a TV star. Big whoop!
I'm starting to think somebody's jealous.
No, I'm not. I don't care that everybody's falling all over him. I care that he's milking it.

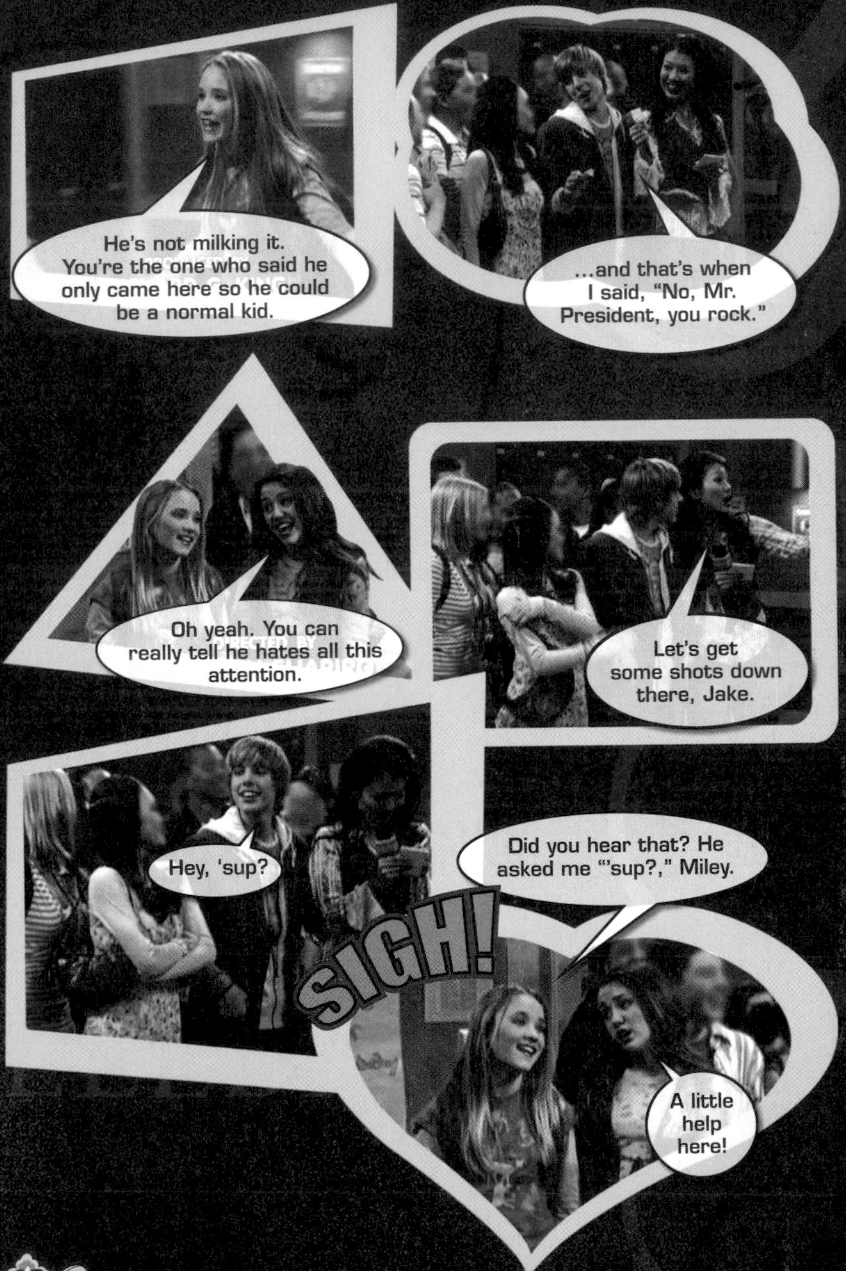
He's not milking it. You're the one who said he only came here so he could be a normal kid.
...and that's when I said, "No, Mr. President, you rock."
Oh yeah. You can really tell he hates all this attention.
Let's get some shots down there, Jake.
Hey, 'sup?
Did you hear that? He asked me "'sup?," Miley.
SIGH!
A little help here!

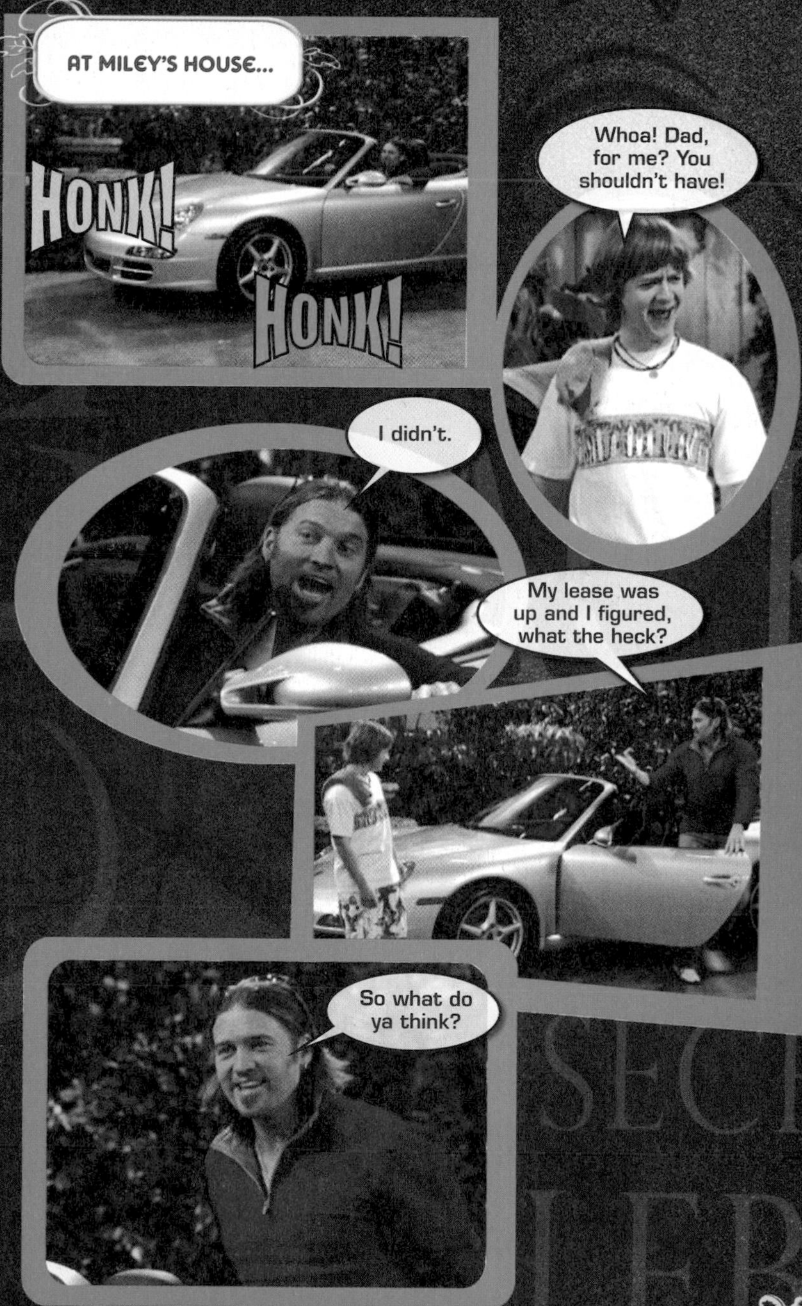
AT MILEY'S HOUSE...
HONK!
HONK!
Whoa! Dad, for me? You shouldn't have!
I didn't.
My lease was up and I figured, what the heck?
So what do ya think?

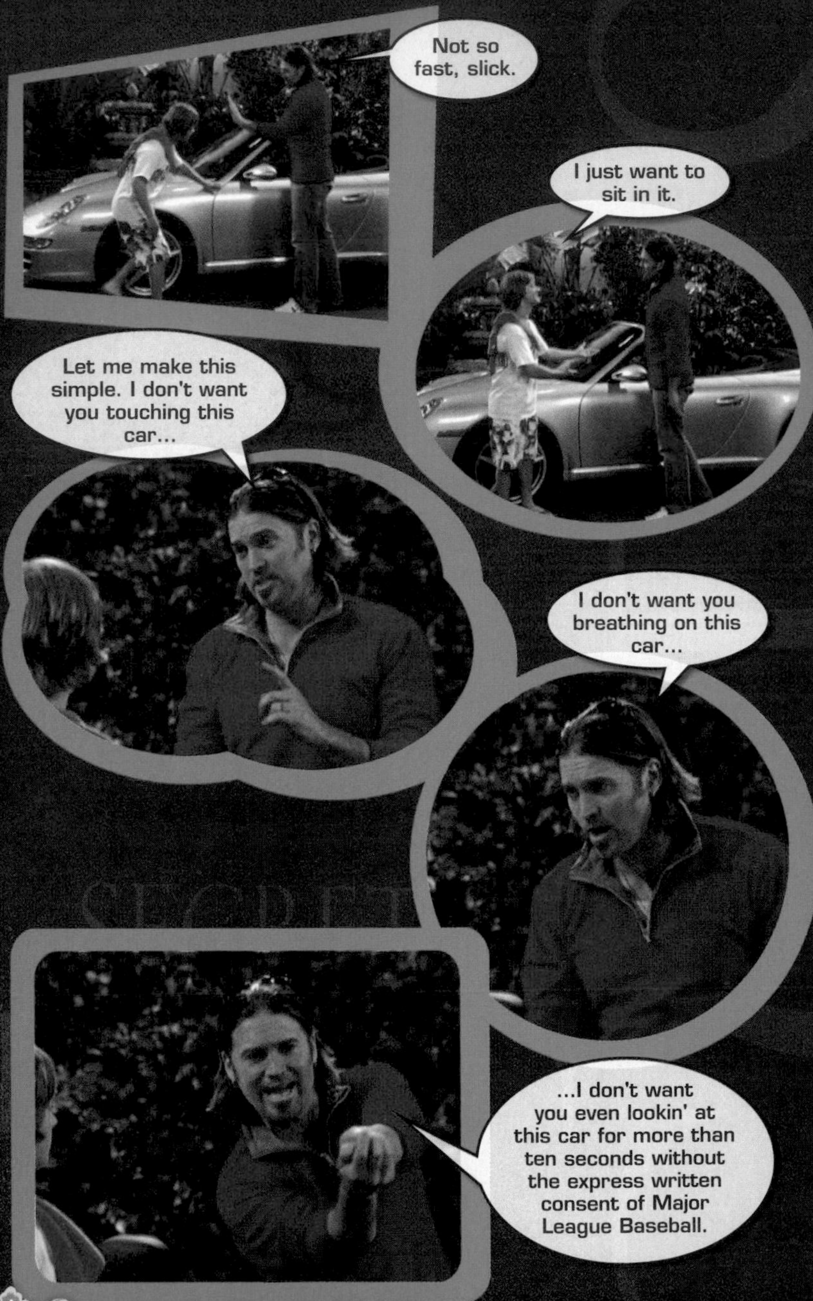
Not so fast, slick.
I just want to sit in it.
Let me make this simple. I don't want you touching this car...
I don't want you breathing on this car...
...I don't want you even lookin' at this car for more than ten seconds without the express written consent of Major League Baseball.

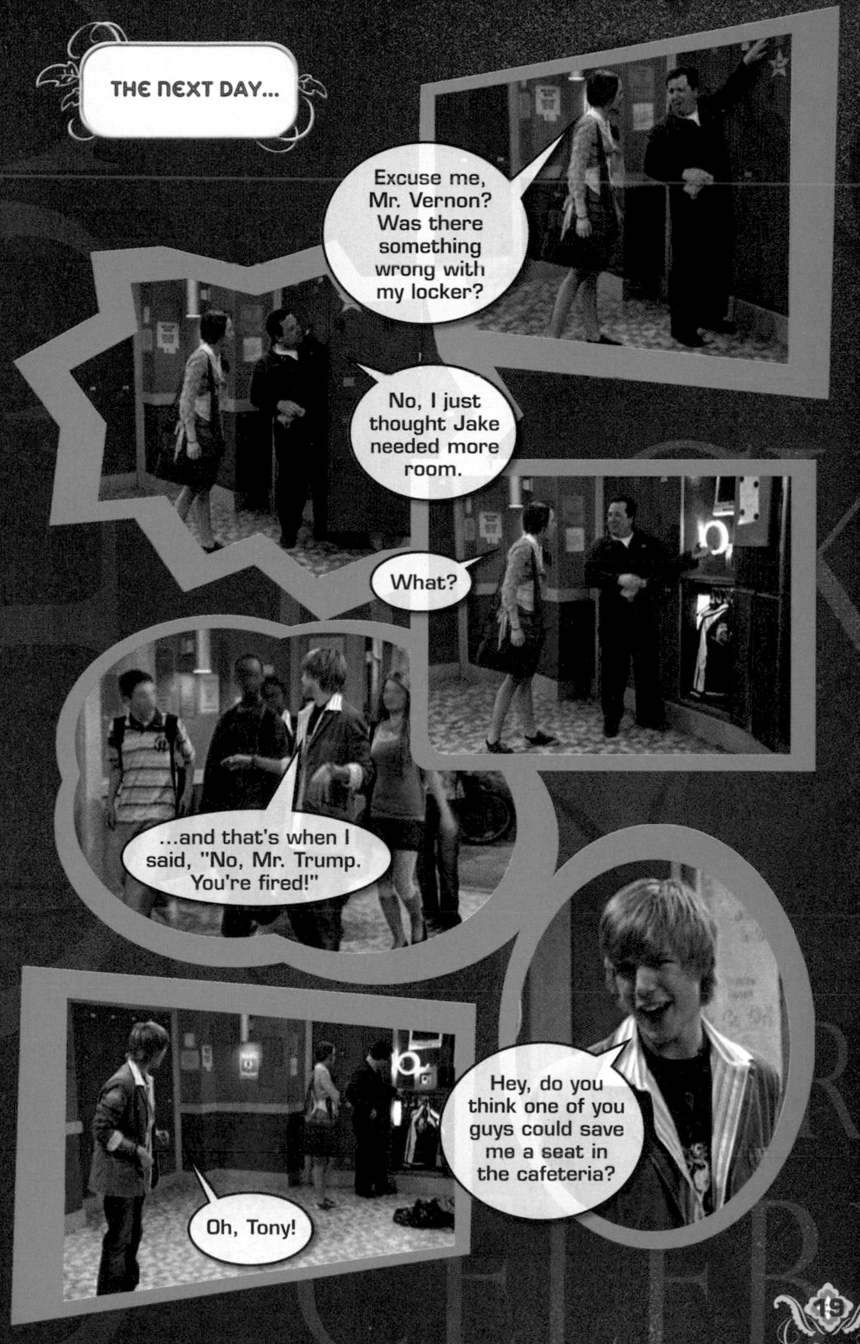
THE NEXT DAY...
Excuse me, Mr. Vernon? Was there something wrong with my locker?
No, I just thought Jake needed more room.
What?
...and that's when I said, "No, Mr. Trump. You're fired!"
Oh, Tony!
Hey, do you think one of you guys could save me a seat in the cafeteria?

I just asked if you could get the squeak out of the door. This is above and beyond.
You da man.
No, you da man.
Oh no, you da man.
No, you da man.
Yeah yeah yeah yeah, great. Who da man who knows where my locker is?

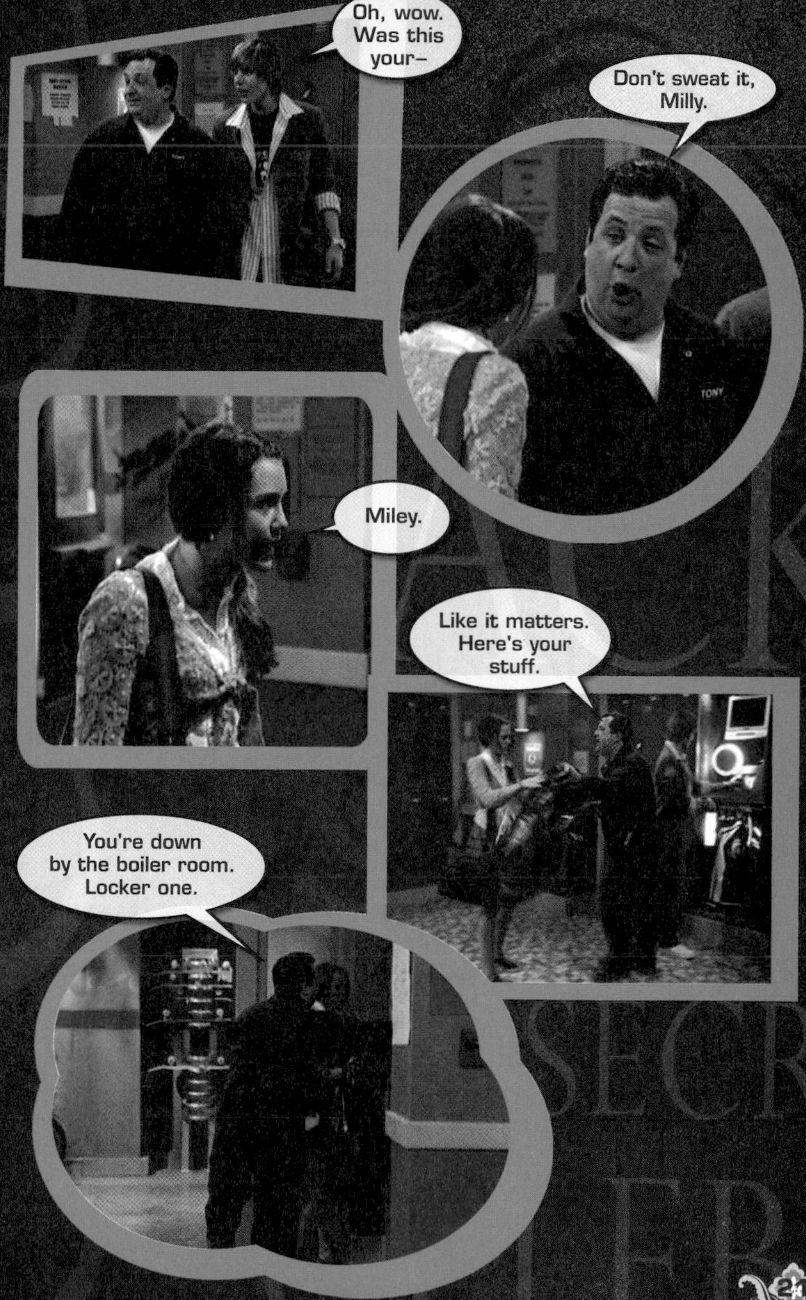
Oh, wow. Was this your–
Don't sweat it, Milly.
Miley.
Like it matters. Here's your stuff.
You're down by the boiler room. Locker one.

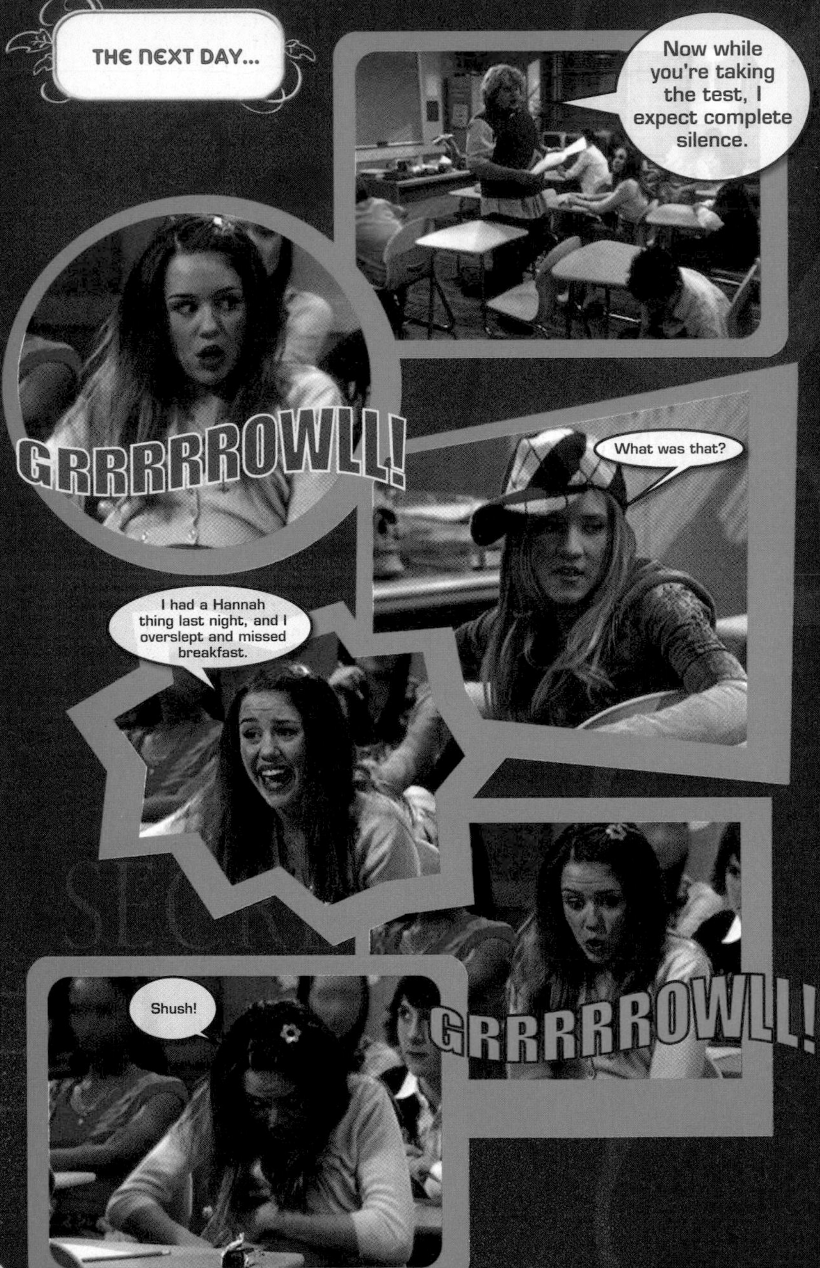
THE NEXT DAY...
Now while you're taking the test, I expect complete silence.
GRRRRROWLL!
What was that?
I had a Hannah thing last night, and I overslept and missed breakfast.
GRRRRROWLL!
Shush!

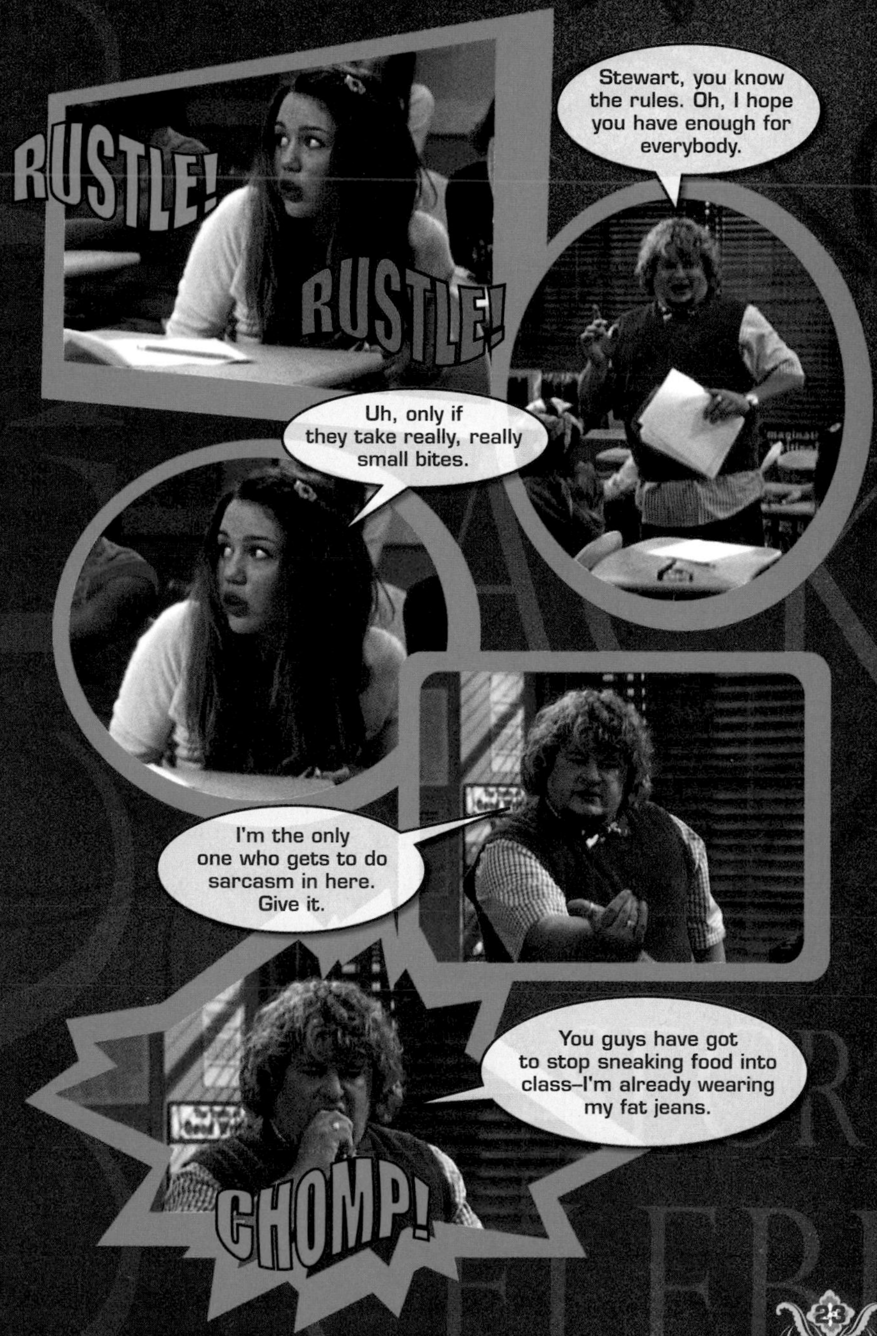
RUSTLE!
RUSTLE!
Stewart, you know the rules. Oh, I hope you have enough for everybody.
Uh, only if they take really, really small bites.
I'm the only one who gets to do sarcasm in here. Give it.
CHOMP!
You guys have got to stop sneaking food into class–I'm already wearing my fat jeans.

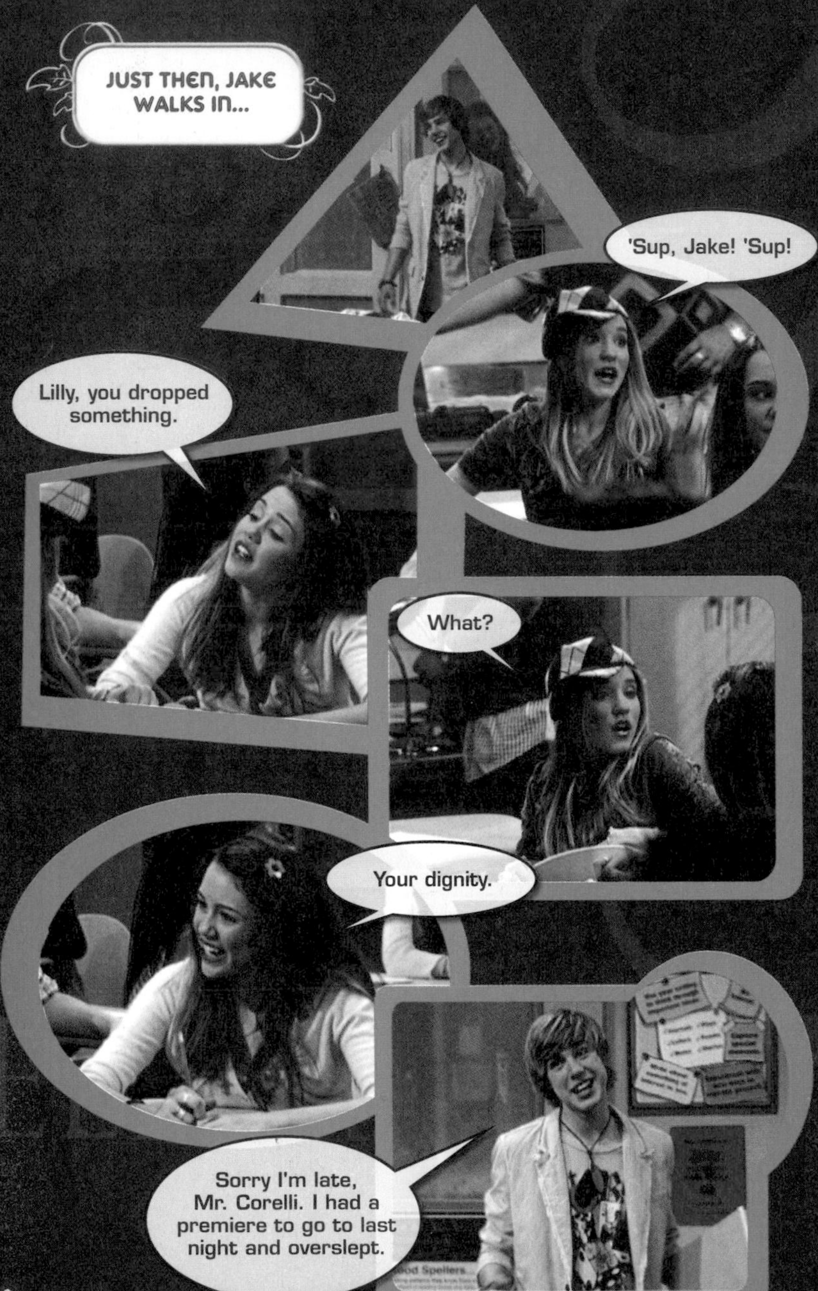
JUST THEN, JAKE WALKS IN...
'Sup, Jake! 'Sup!
Lilly, you dropped something.
What?
Your dignity.
Sorry I'm late, Mr. Corelli. I had a premiere to go to last night and overslept.

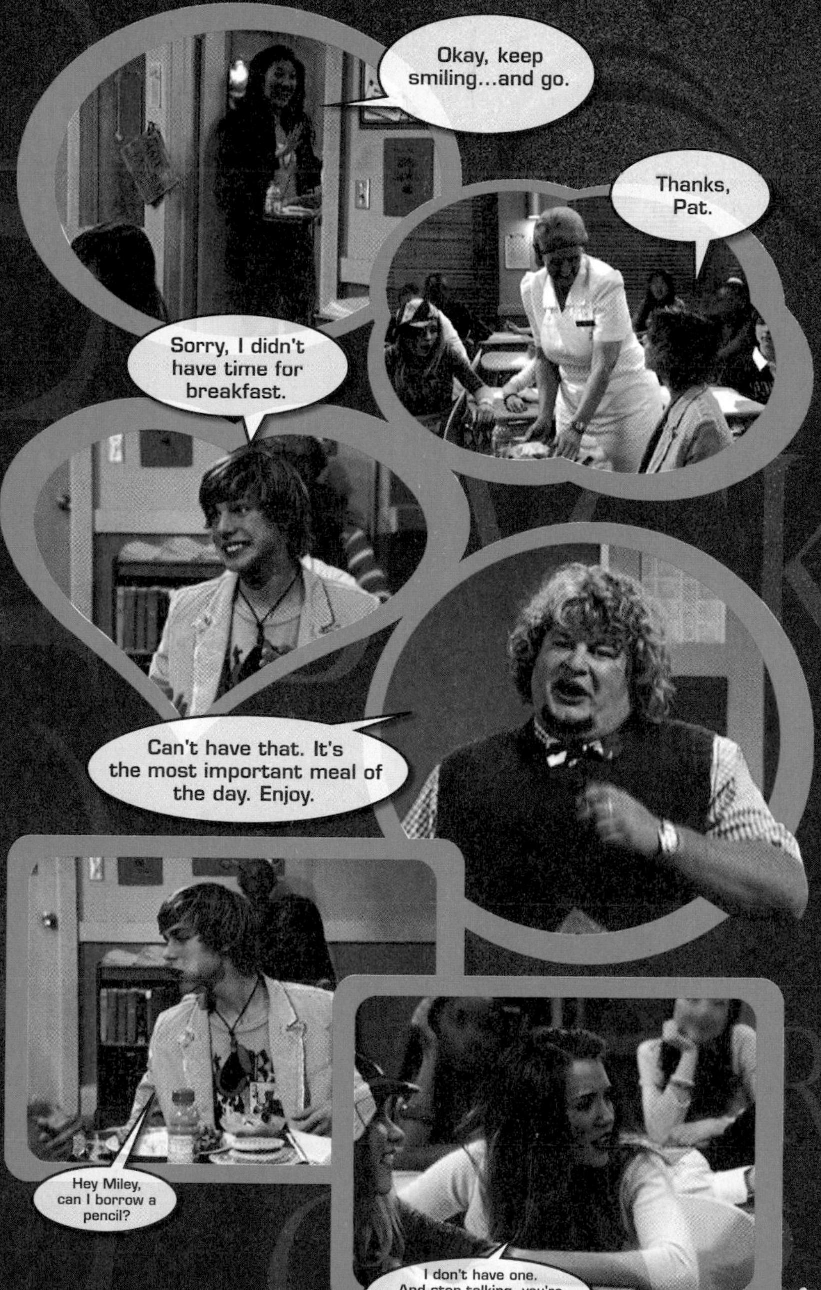
Okay, keep smiling...and go.
Thanks, Pat.
Sorry, I didn't have time for breakfast.
Can't have that. It's the most important meal of the day. Enjoy.
Hey Miley, can I borrow a pencil?
I don't have one. And stop talking, you're gonna get us in trouble.

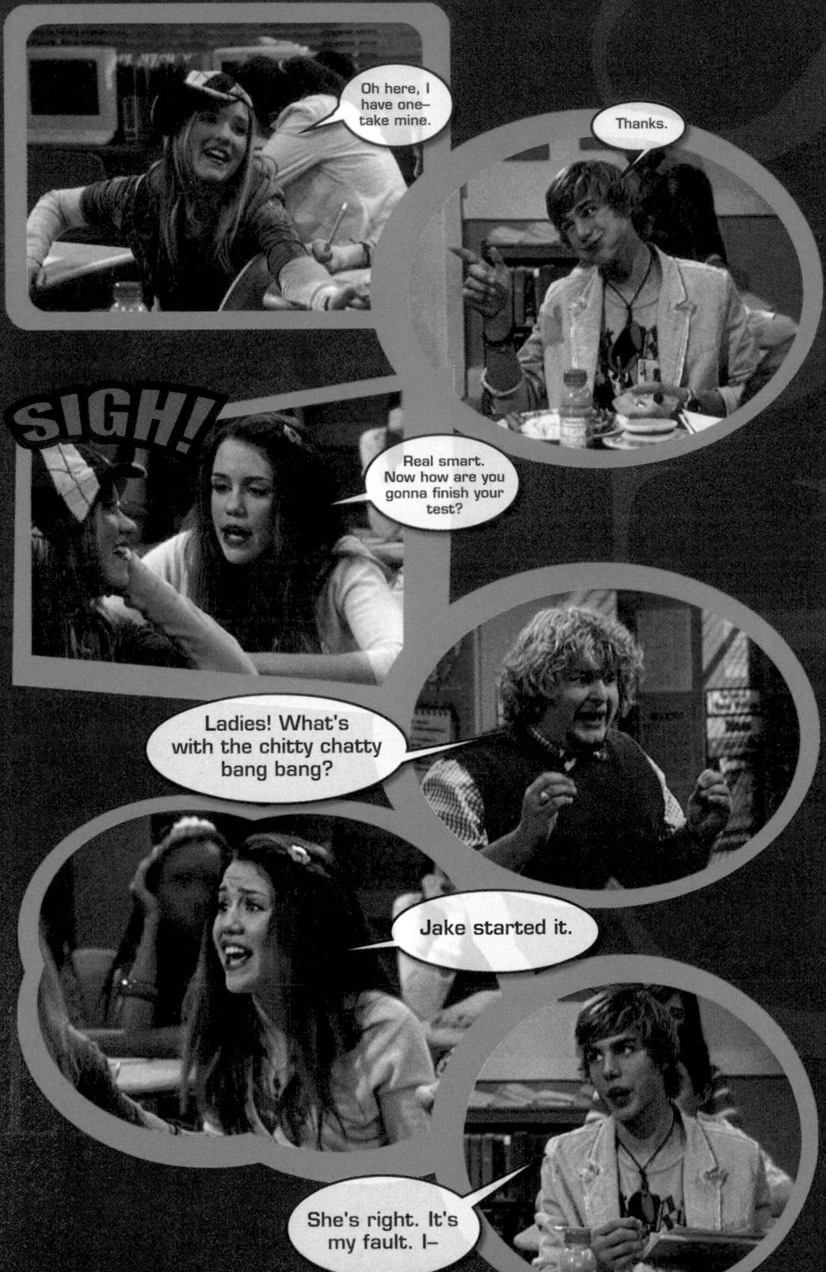
Oh here, I have one– take mine.
Thanks.
SIGH!
Real smart. Now how are you gonna finish your test?
Ladies! What's with the chitty chatty bang bang?
Jake started it.
She's right. It's my fault. I–

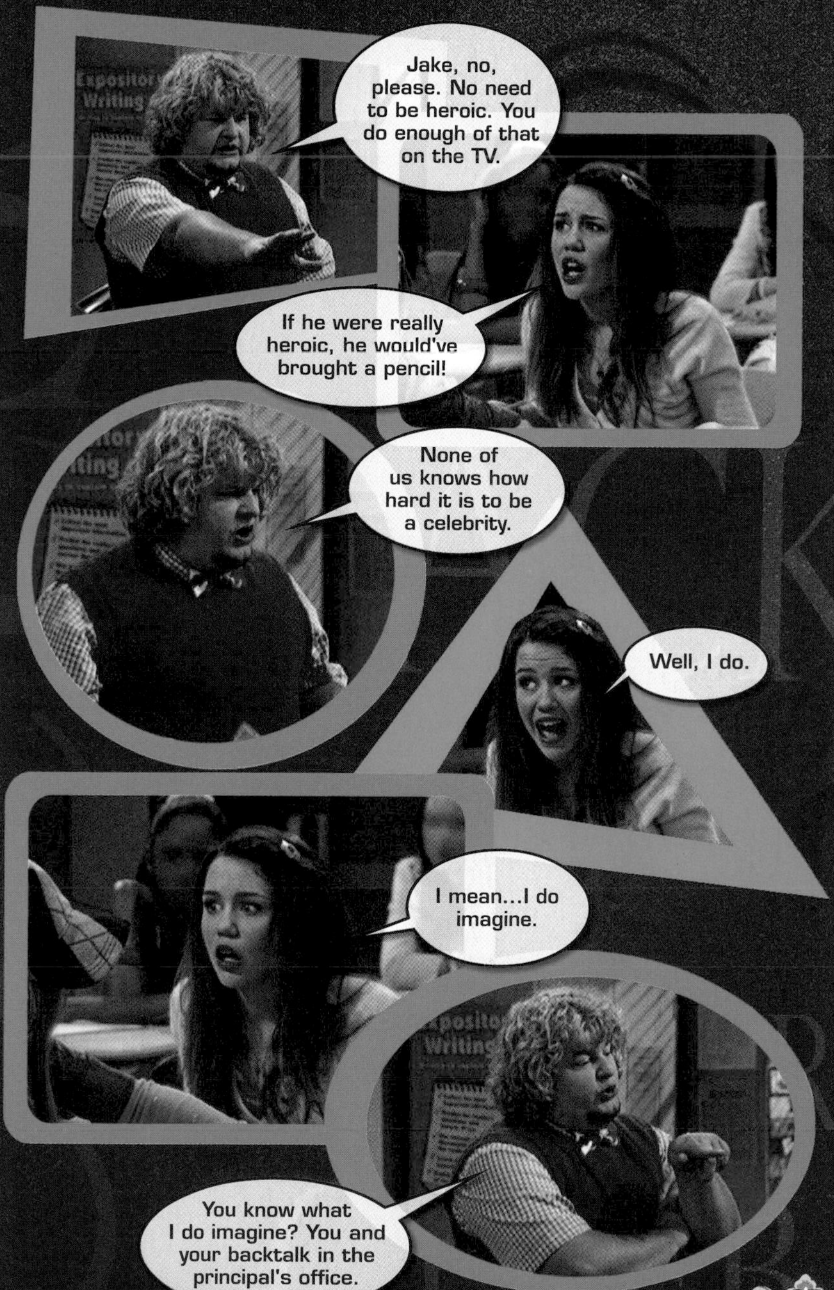
Jake, no, please. No need to be heroic. You do enough of that on the TV.
If he were really heroic, he would've brought a pencil!
None of us knows how hard it is to be a celebrity.
Well, I do.
I mean...I do imagine.
You know what I do imagine? You and your backtalk in the principal's office.

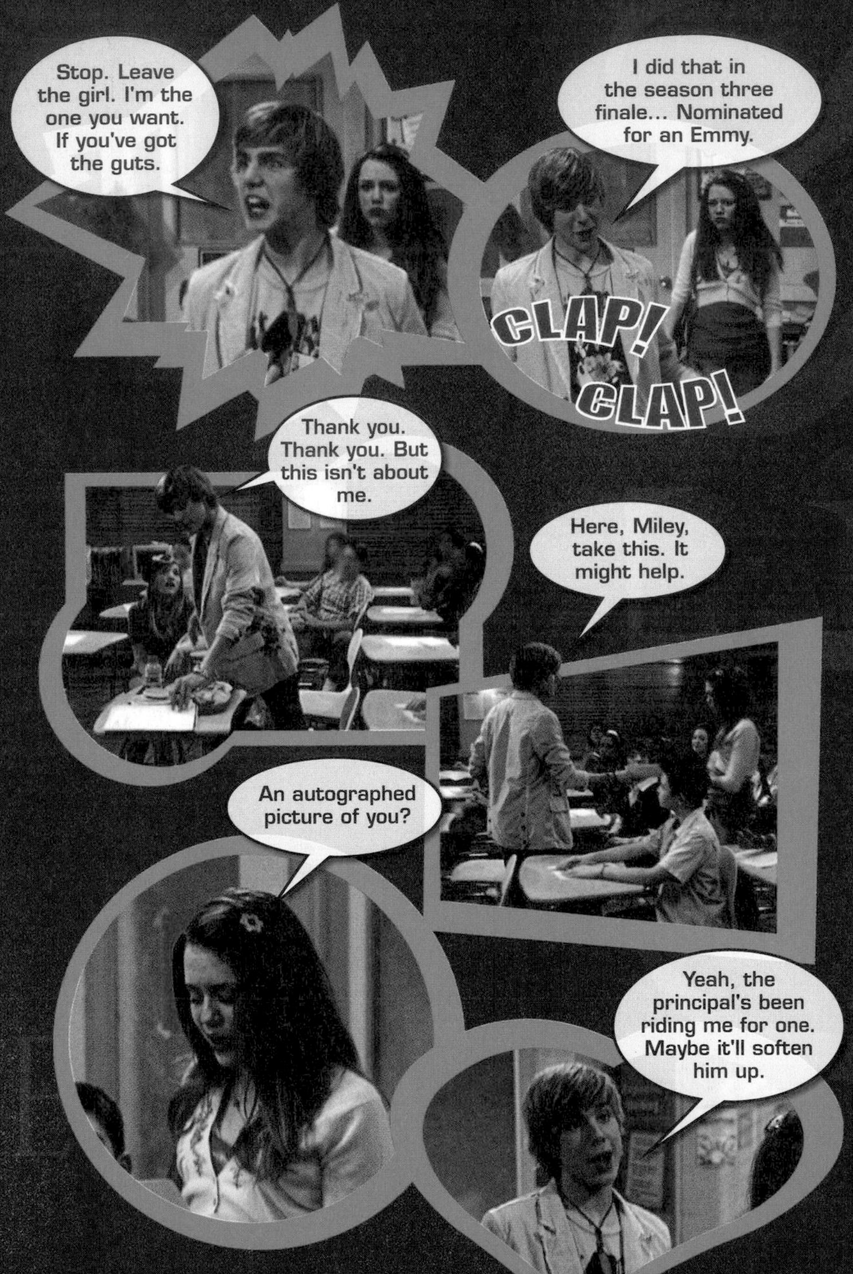
Stop. Leave the girl. I'm the one you want. If you've got the guts.
I did that in the season three finale... Nominated for an Emmy.
CLAP! CLAP!
Thank you. Thank you. But this isn't about me.
Here, Miley, take this. It might help.
An autographed picture of you?
Yeah, the principal's been riding me for one. Maybe it'll soften him up.

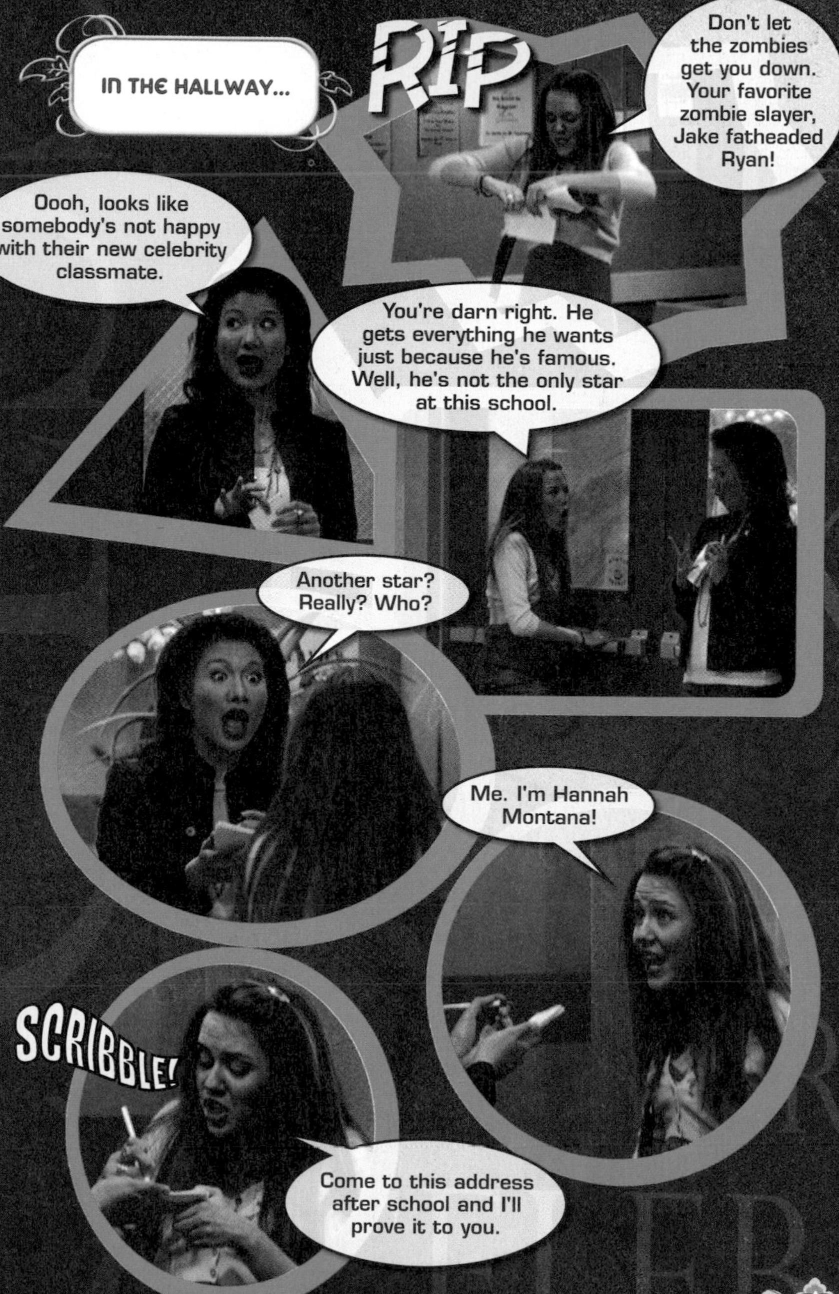
IN THE HALLWAY...
RIP
Don't let the zombies get you down. Your favorite zombie slayer, Jake fatheaded Ryan!
Oooh, looks like somebody's not happy with their new celebrity classmate.
You're darn right. He gets everything he wants just because he's famous. Well, he's not the only star at this school.
Another star? Really? Who?
Me. I'm Hannah Montana!
SCRIBBLE!
Come to this address after school and I'll prove it to you.

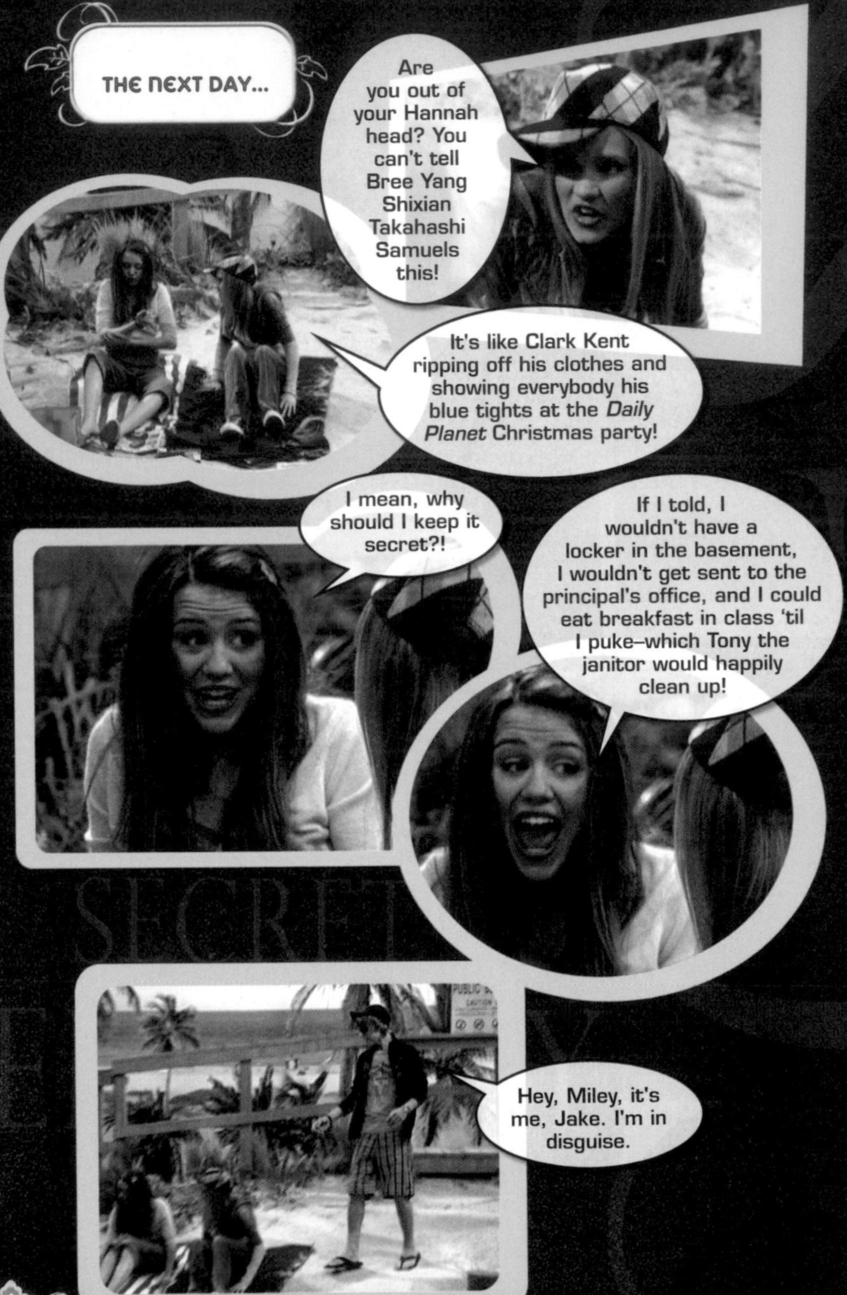
THE NEXT DAY...
Are you out of your Hannah head? You can't tell Bree Yang Shixian Takahashi Samuels this!
It's like Clark Kent ripping off his clothes and showing everybody his blue tights at the *Daily Planet* Christmas party!
I mean, why should I keep it secret?!
If I told, I wouldn't have a locker in the basement, I wouldn't get sent to the principal's office, and I could eat breakfast in class 'til I puke–which Tony the janitor would happily clean up!
Hey, Miley, it's me, Jake. I'm in disguise.

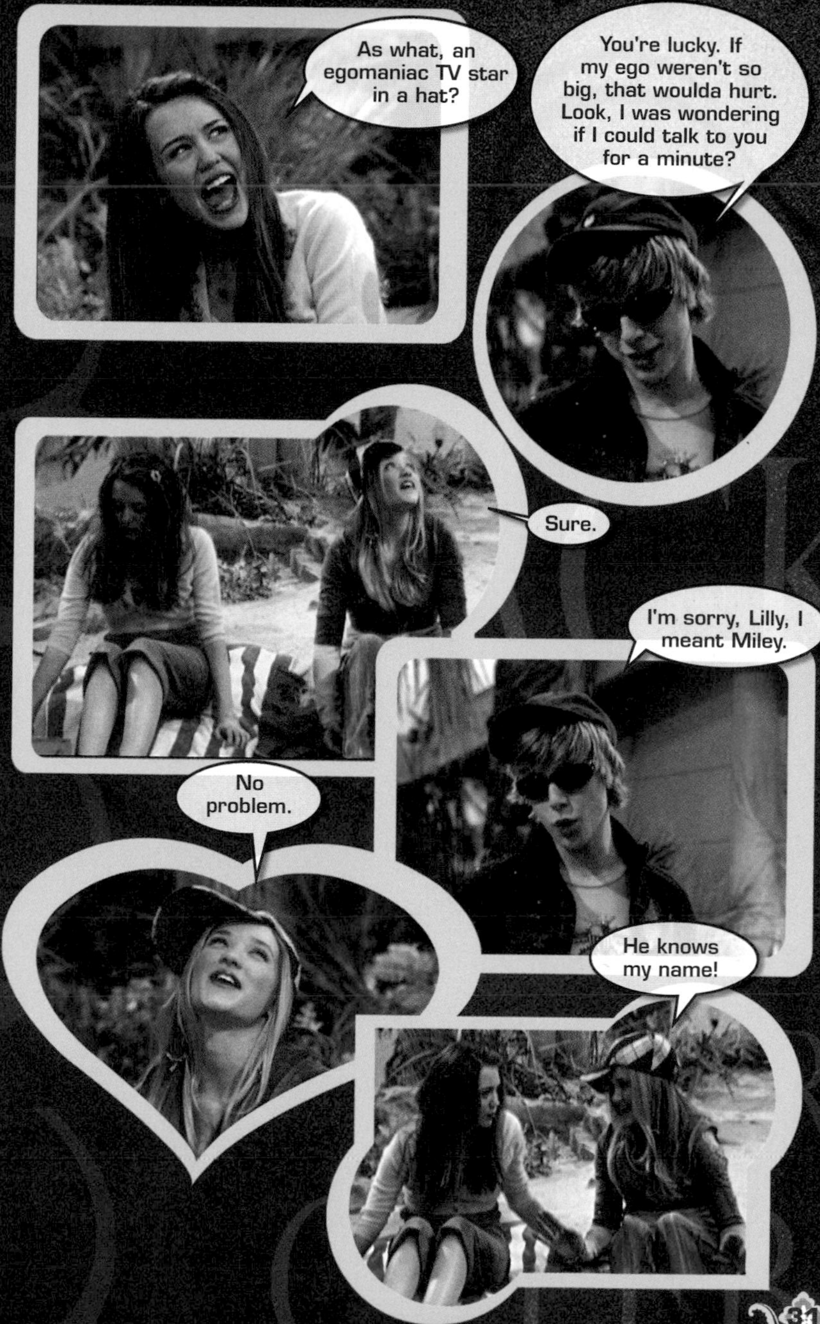
As what, an egomaniac TV star in a hat?
You're lucky. If my ego weren't so big, that woulda hurt. Look, I was wondering if I could talk to you for a minute?
Sure.
I'm sorry, Lilly, I meant Miley.
No problem.
He knows my name!

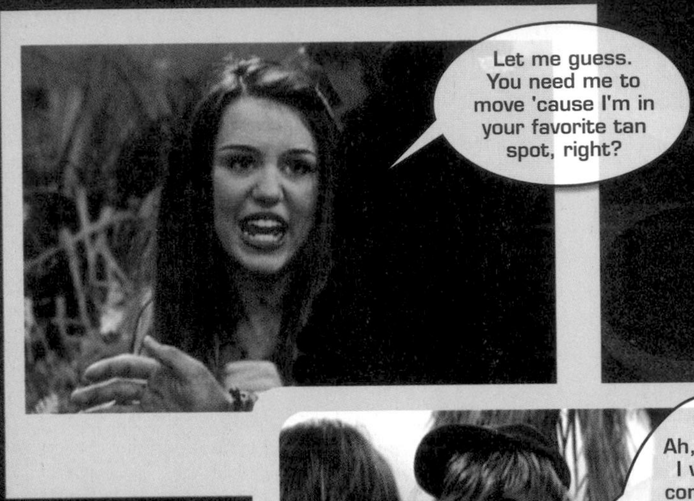
Let me guess. You need me to move 'cause I'm in your favorite tan spot, right?

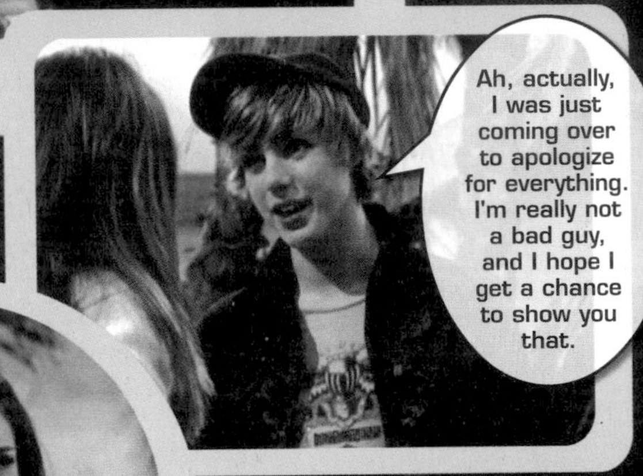
Ah, actually, I was just coming over to apologize for everything. I'm really not a bad guy, and I hope I get a chance to show you that.

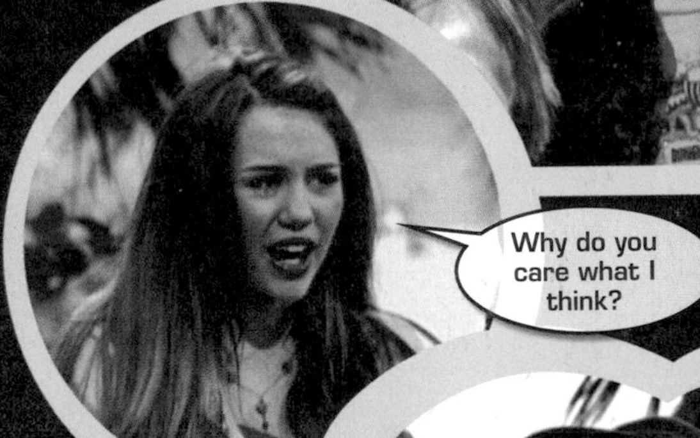
Why do you care what I think?

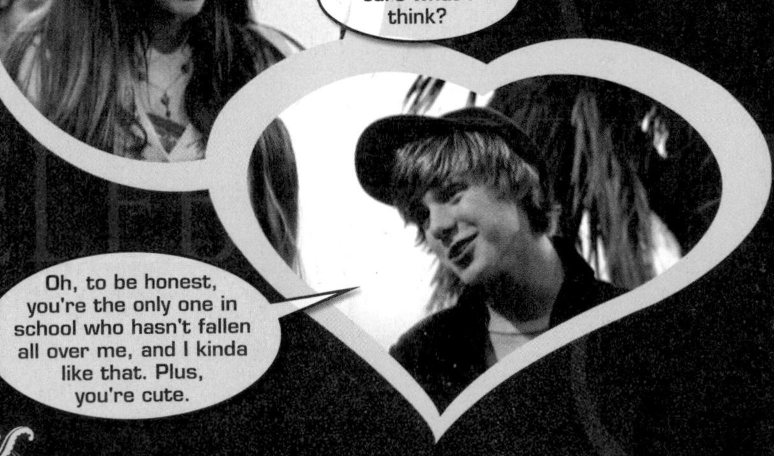
Oh, to be honest, you're the only one in school who hasn't fallen all over me, and I kinda like that. Plus, you're cute.

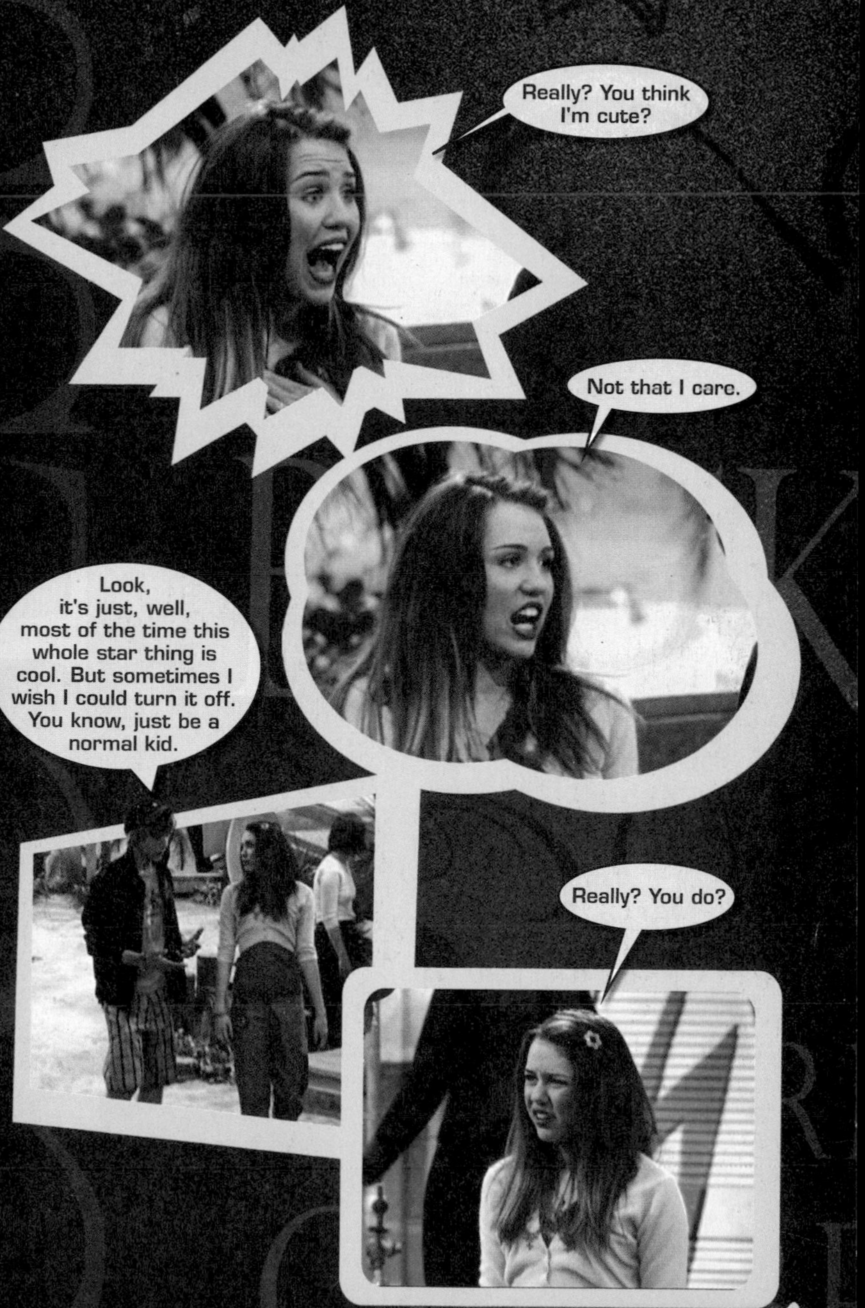
Really? You think I'm cute?
Not that I care.
Look, it's just, well, most of the time this whole star thing is cool. But sometimes I wish I could turn it off. You know, just be a normal kid.
Really? You do?

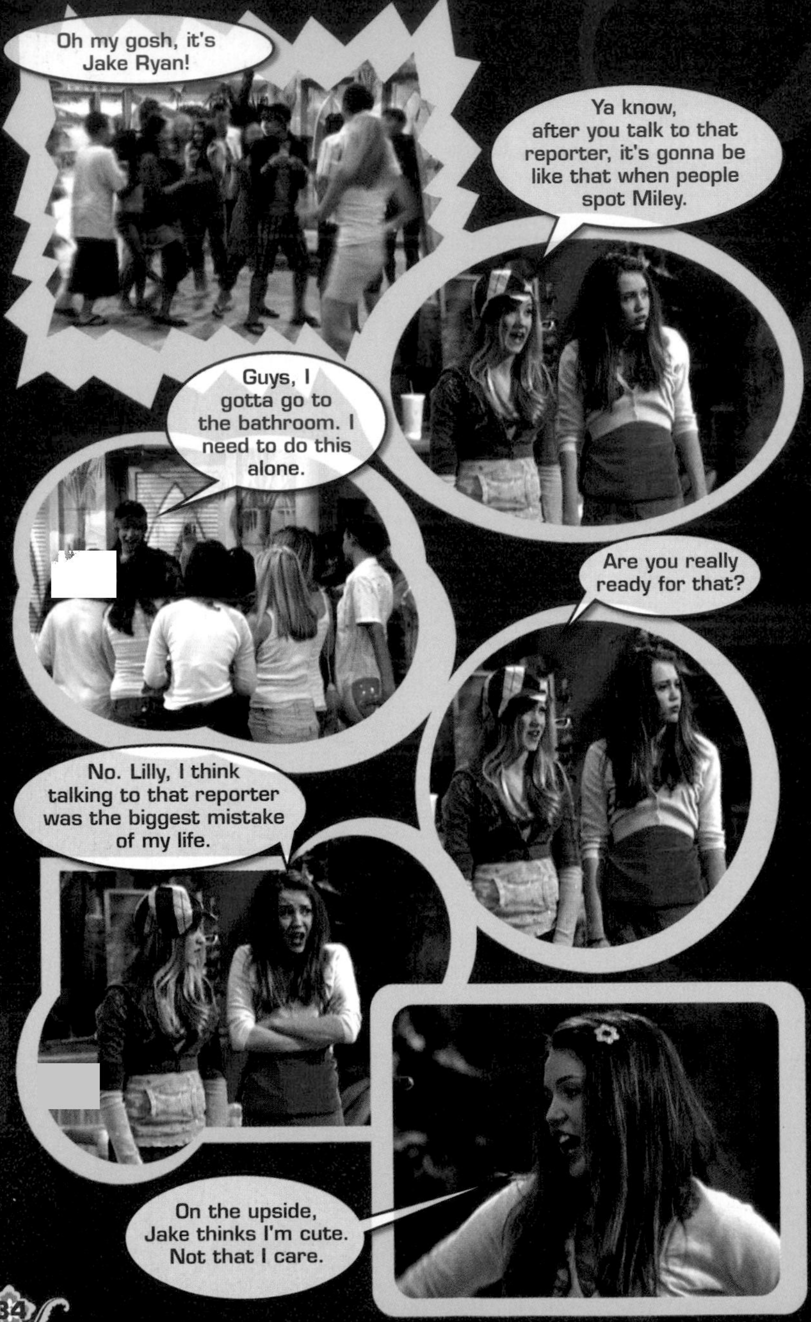
Oh my gosh, it's Jake Ryan!
Ya know, after you talk to that reporter, it's gonna be like that when people spot Miley.
Guys, I gotta go to the bathroom. I need to do this alone.
Are you really ready for that?
No. Lilly, I think talking to that reporter was the biggest mistake of my life.
On the upside, Jake thinks I'm cute. Not that I care.

Sounds like a dead battery, son.

Start!

It can't be. I have to pick up Jennifer for the Coldplay concert. Turn over, you piece of junk! No, I'm sorry, I didn't mean that, baby.

Son, you can apologize all you want, but without a new battery, you'd have an easier time turning over Uncle Earl on his waterbed.

Hey Dad, do you think maybe I could, ah...

No.

35

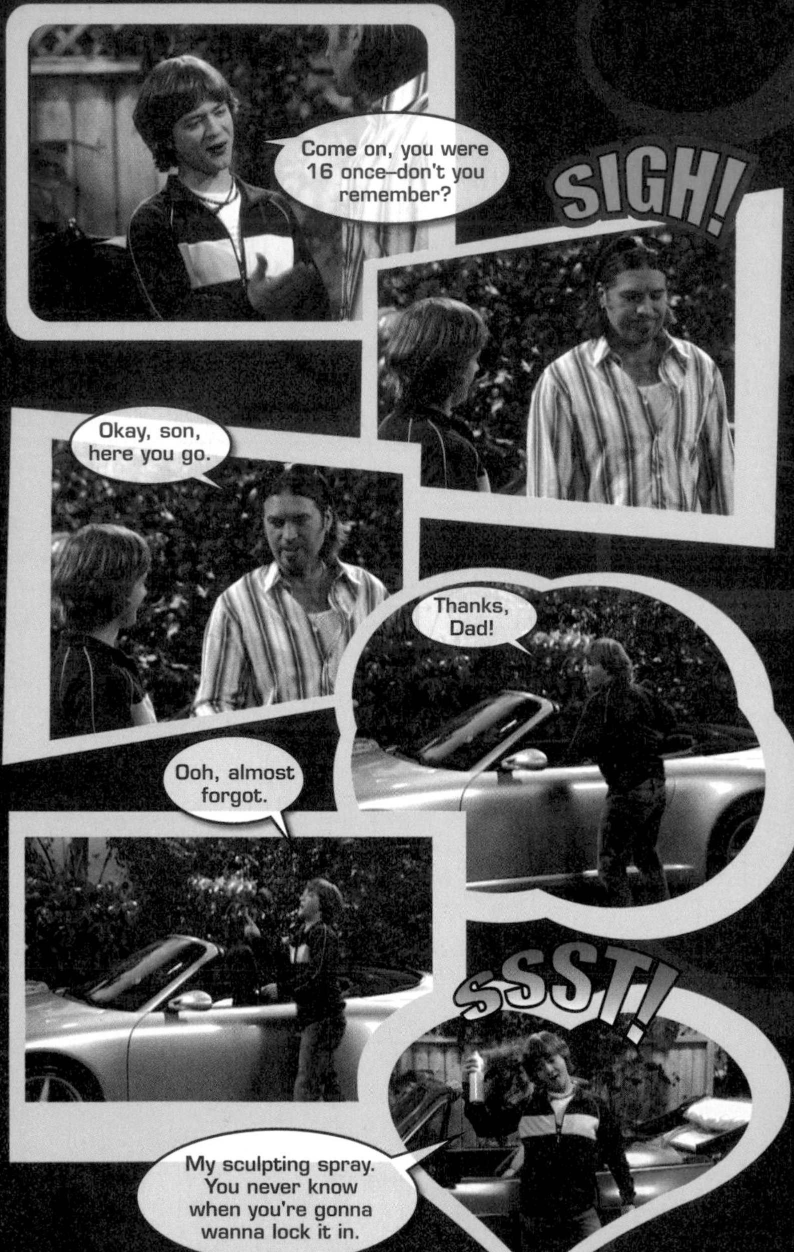
Come on, you were 16 once–don't you remember?
SIGH!
Okay, son, here you go.
Thanks, Dad!
Ooh, almost forgot.
SSST!
My sculpting spray. You never know when you're gonna wanna lock it in.

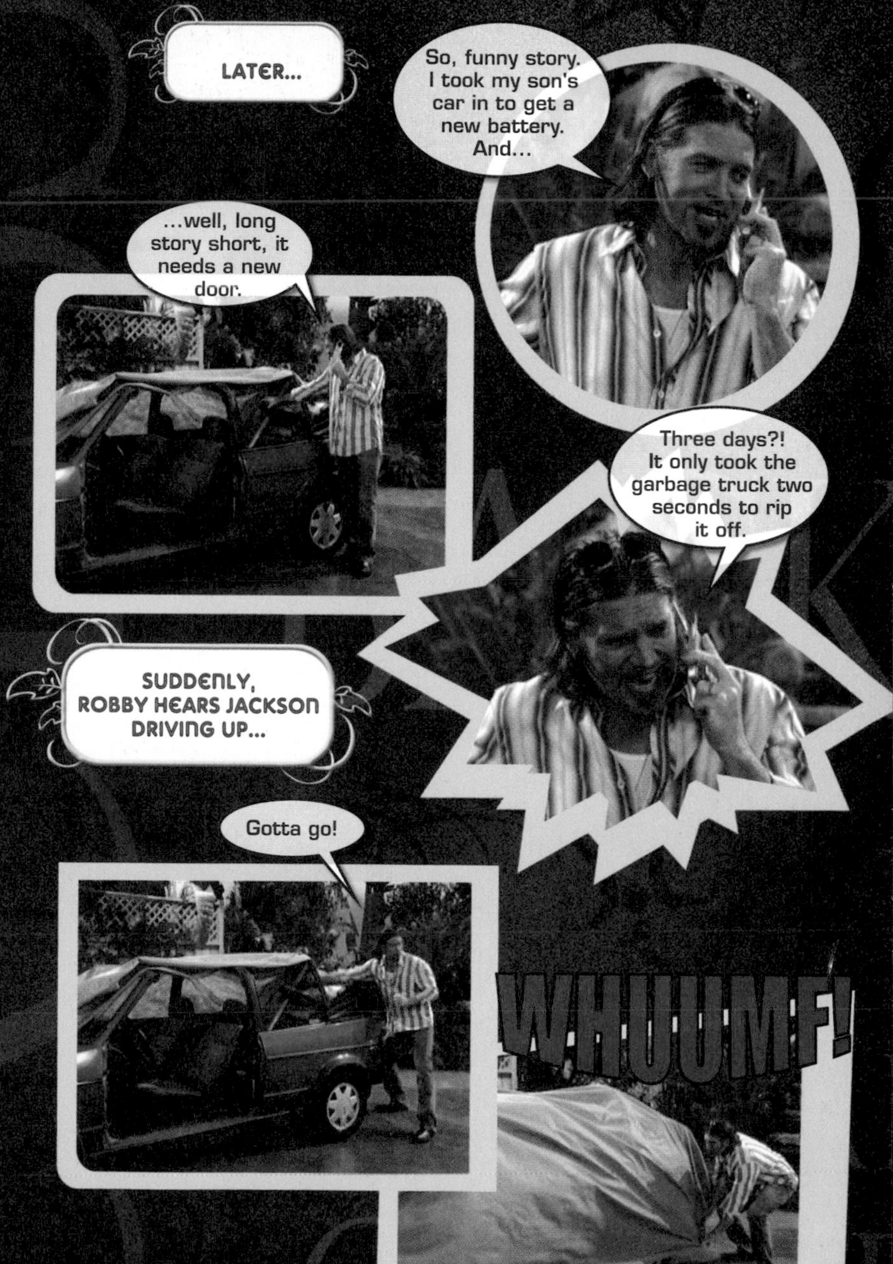
LATER...
So, funny story. I took my son's car in to get a new battery. And...
...well, long story short, it needs a new door.
Three days?! It only took the garbage truck two seconds to rip it off.
SUDDENLY, ROBBY HEARS JACKSON DRIVING UP...
Gotta go!
WHUUMF!

So, son, whatcha doin' home so soon? Coldplay catch a cold? Get it? C'mon, let's go in the house.
No, wait, Dad. I have to tell you something about the car.
Oh, your car's fine. Got a new battery for it. My gift to you. Come on, let's go on in the house and wrestle like we used to.
It's not my car. Yours. Something happened.
...What?
Well, when I was going to pick up Jennifer, her dad brought out the Rottweiler to make sure the dog had my scent. And one of the spikes on his collar kind of...well...

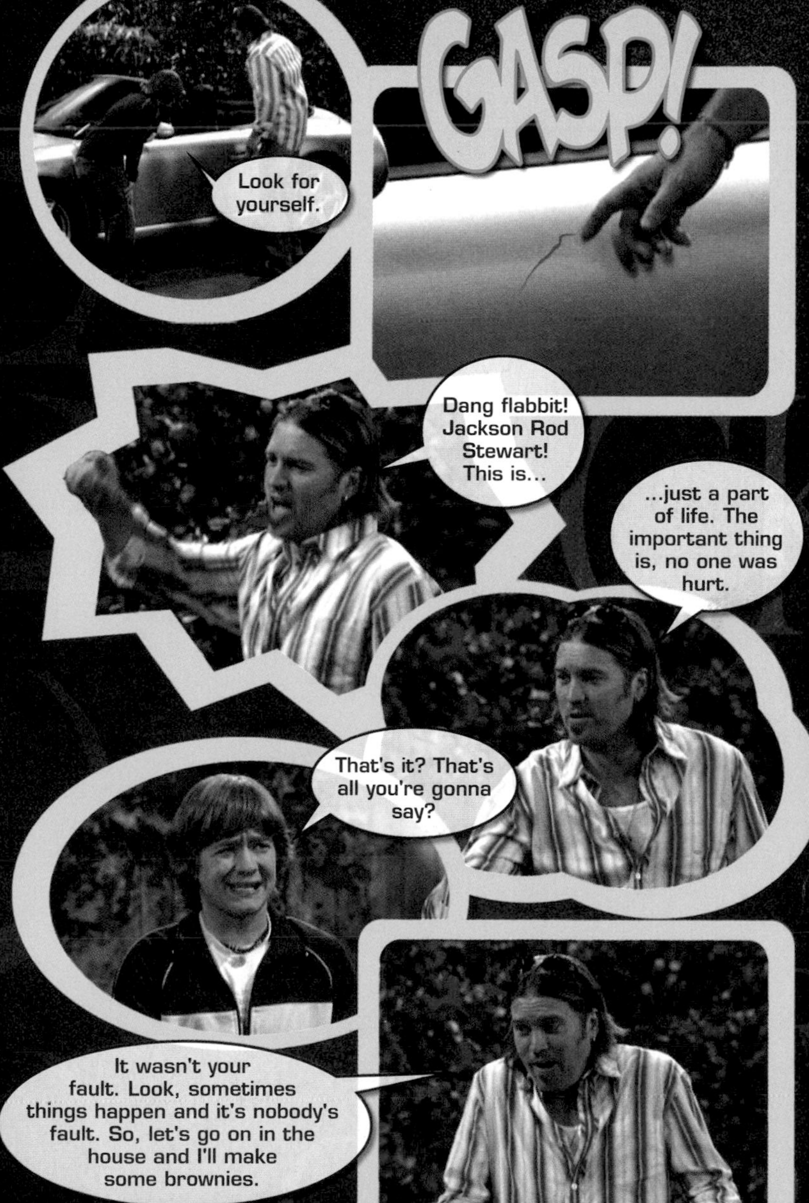
Look for yourself.
GASP!
Dang flabbit! Jackson Rod Stewart! This is...
...just a part of life. The important thing is, no one was hurt.
That's it? That's all you're gonna say?
It wasn't your fault. Look, sometimes things happen and it's nobody's fault. So, let's go on in the house and I'll make some brownies.

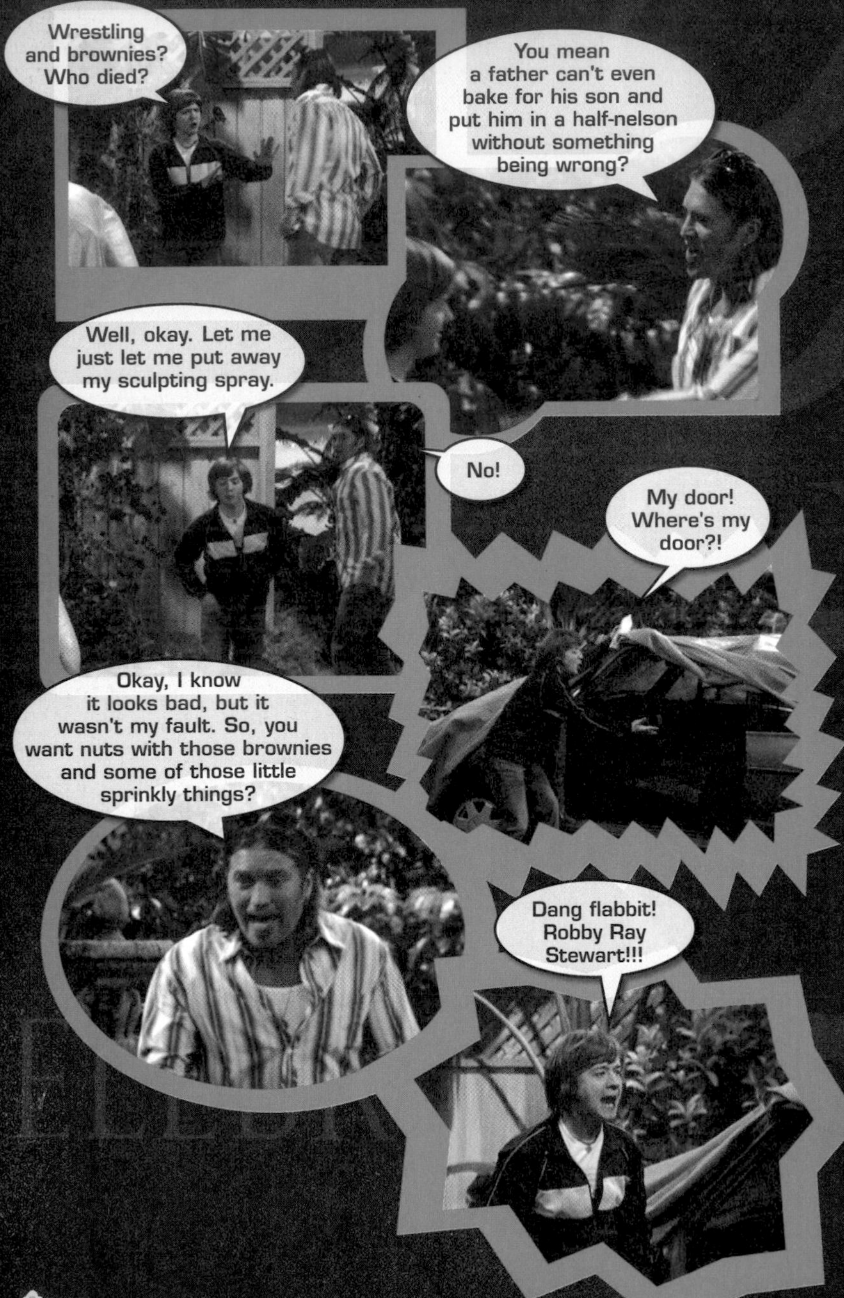
Wrestling and brownies? Who died?
You mean a father can't even bake for his son and put him in a half-nelson without something being wrong?
Well, okay. Let me just let me put away my sculpting spray.
No!
My door! Where's my door?!
Okay, I know it looks bad, but it wasn't my fault. So, you want nuts with those brownies and some of those little sprinkly things?
Dang flabbit! Robby Ray Stewart!!!

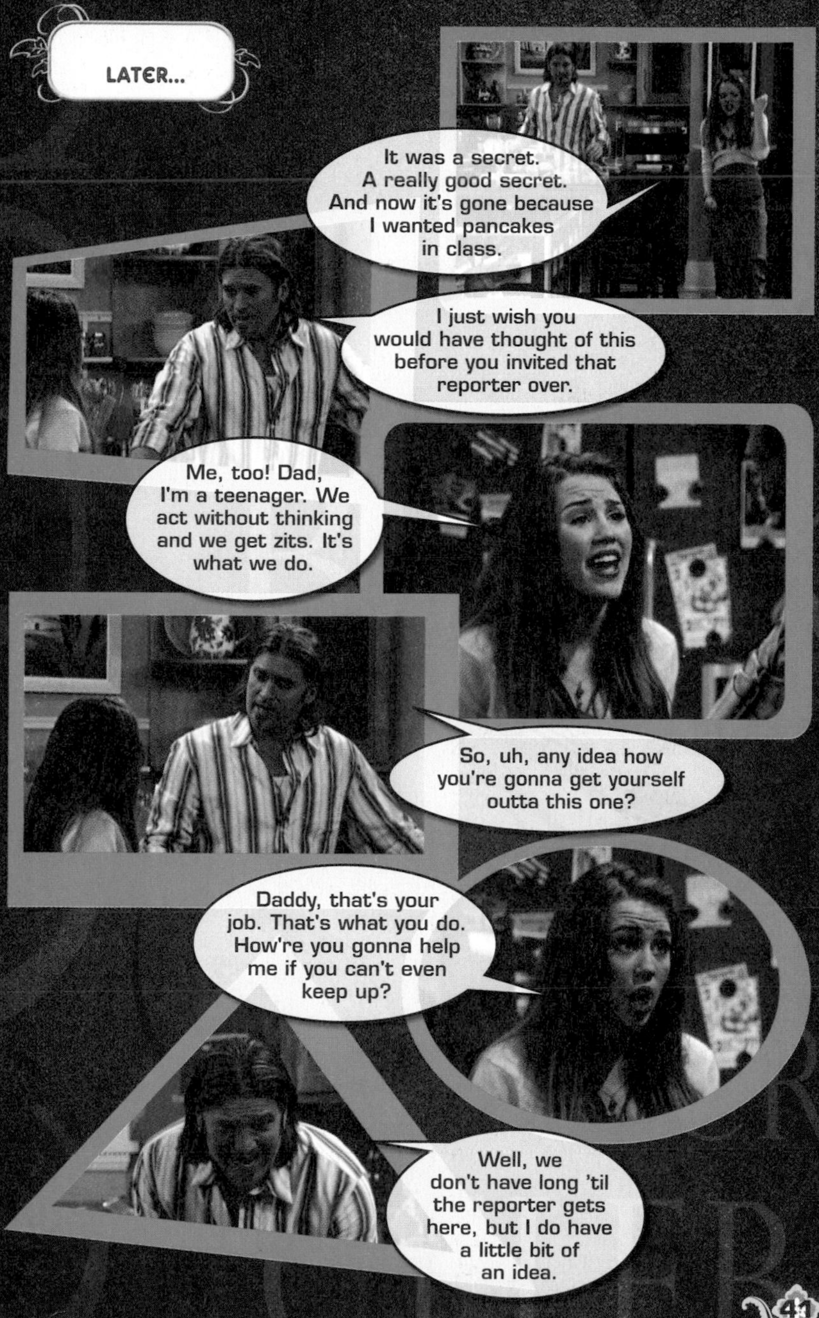
LATER...
It was a secret. A really good secret. And now it's gone because I wanted pancakes in class.
I just wish you would have thought of this before you invited that reporter over.
Me, too! Dad, I'm a teenager. We act without thinking and we get zits. It's what we do.
So, uh, any idea how you're gonna get yourself outta this one?
Daddy, that's your job. That's what you do. How're you gonna help me if you can't even keep up?
Well, we don't have long 'til the reporter gets here, but I do have a little bit of an idea.

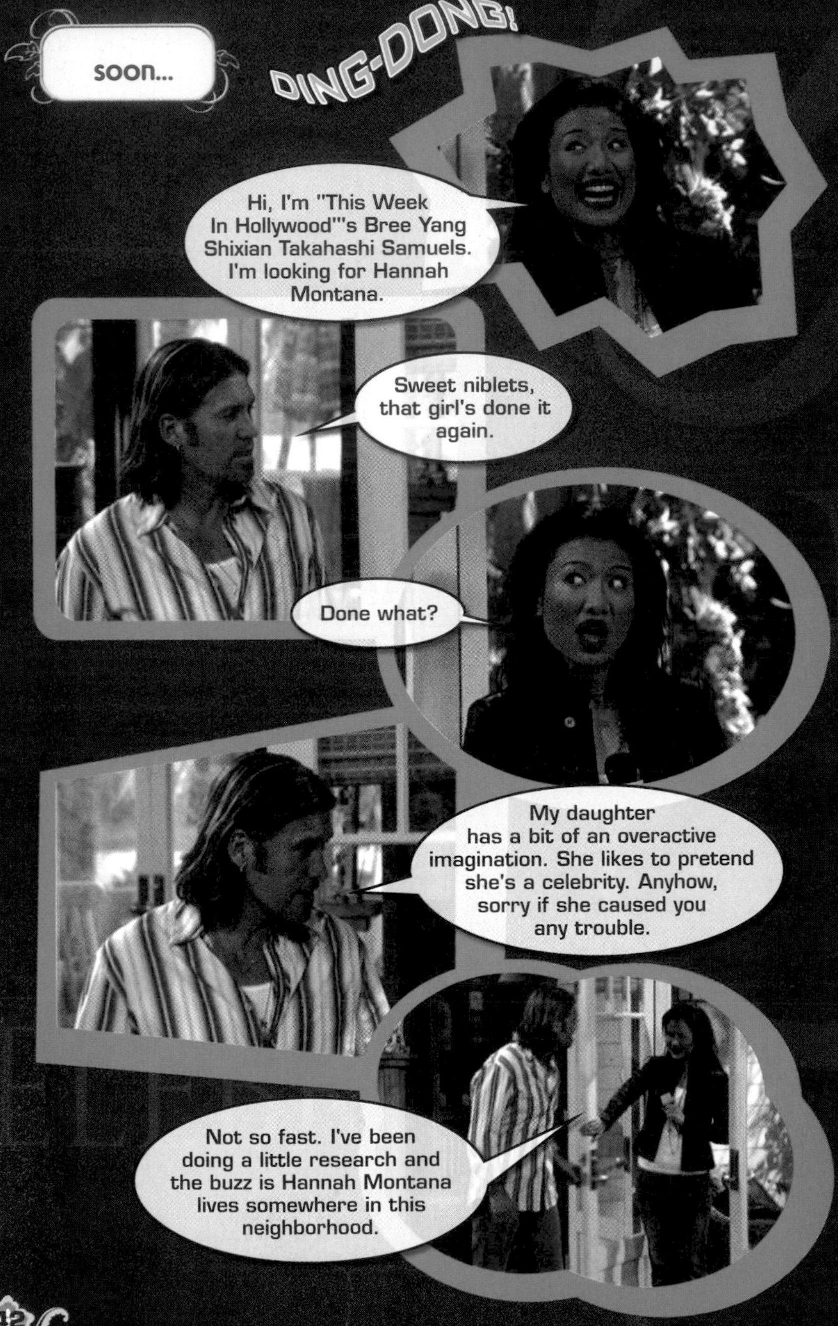
soon...
DING-DONG!
Hi, I'm "This Week In Hollywood"'s Bree Yang Shixian Takahashi Samuels. I'm looking for Hannah Montana.
Sweet niblets, that girl's done it again.
Done what?
My daughter has a bit of an overactive imagination. She likes to pretend she's a celebrity. Anyhow, sorry if she caused you any trouble.
Not so fast. I've been doing a little research and the buzz is Hannah Montana lives somewhere in this neighborhood.

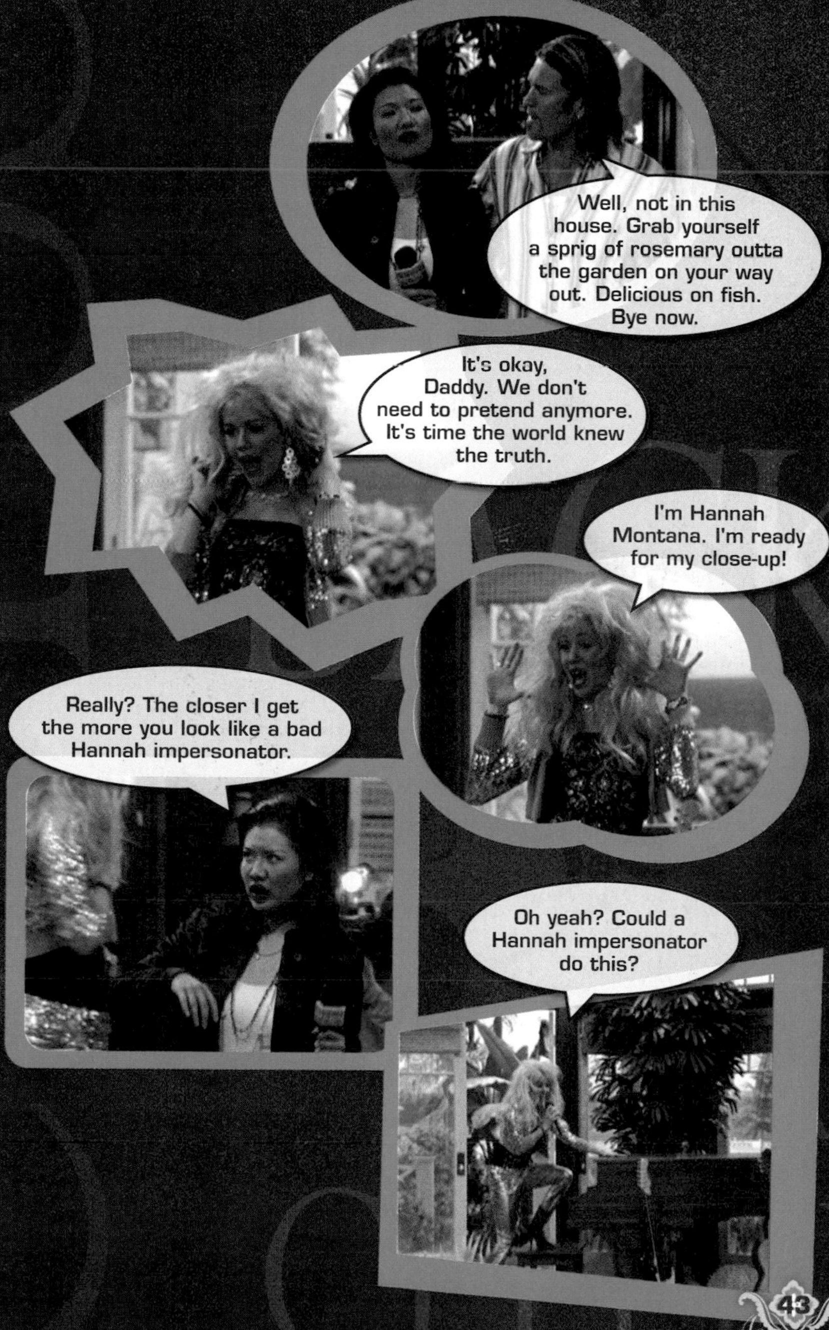
Well, not in this house. Grab yourself a sprig of rosemary outta the garden on your way out. Delicious on fish. Bye now.
It's okay, Daddy. We don't need to pretend anymore. It's time the world knew the truth.
I'm Hannah Montana. I'm ready for my close-up!
Really? The closer I get the more you look like a bad Hannah impersonator.
Oh yeah? Could a Hannah impersonator do this?

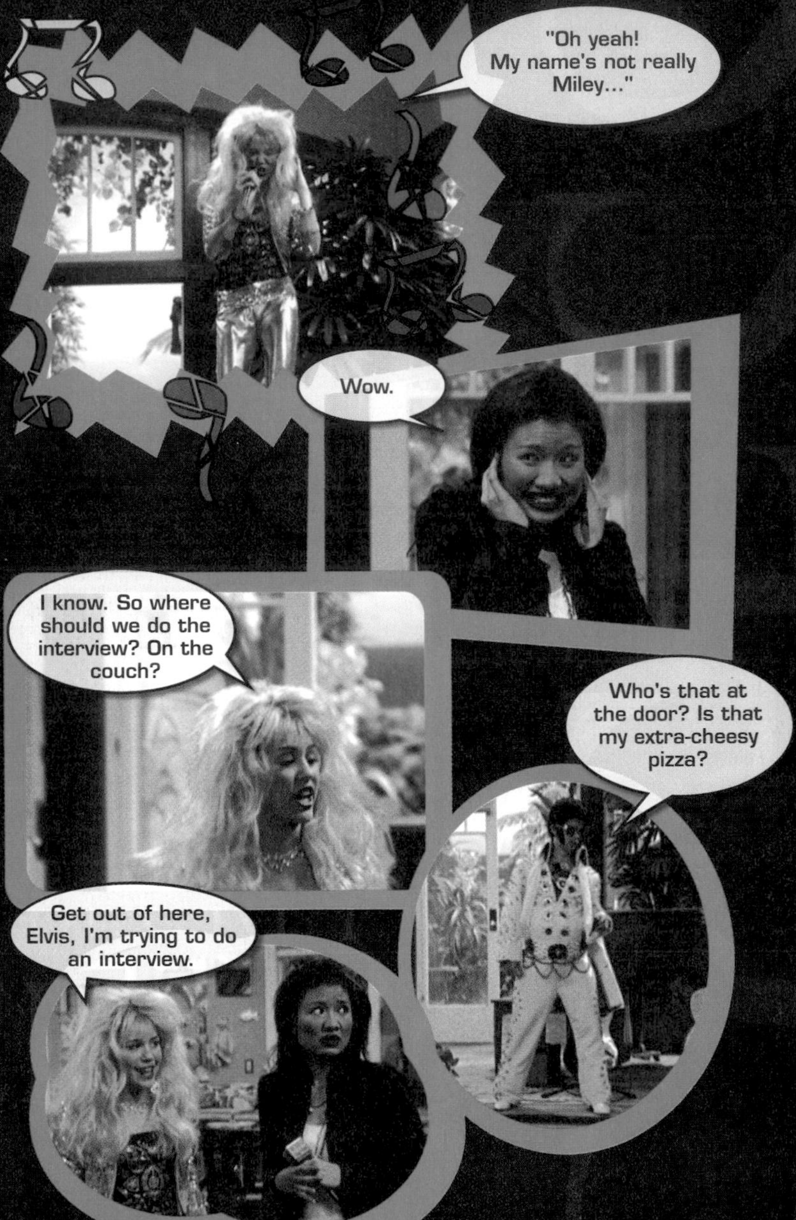
"Oh yeah! My name's not really Miley..."
Wow.
I know. So where should we do the interview? On the couch?
Who's that at the door? Is that my extra-cheesy pizza?
Get out of here, Elvis, I'm trying to do an interview.

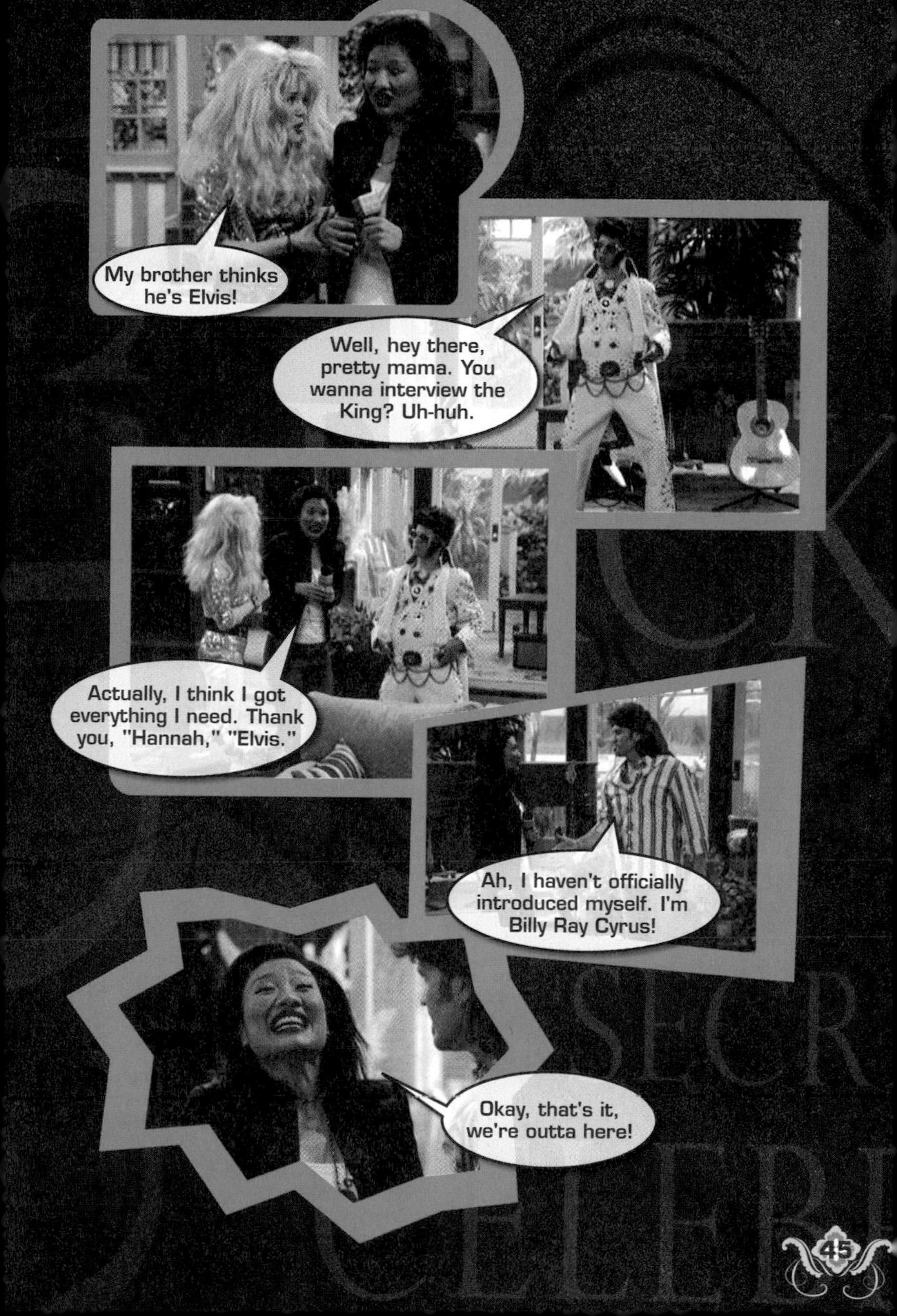
My brother thinks he's Elvis!
Well, hey there, pretty mama. You wanna interview the King? Uh-huh.
Actually, I think I got everything I need. Thank you, "Hannah," "Elvis."
Ah, I haven't officially introduced myself. I'm Billy Ray Cyrus!
Okay, that's it, we're outta here!

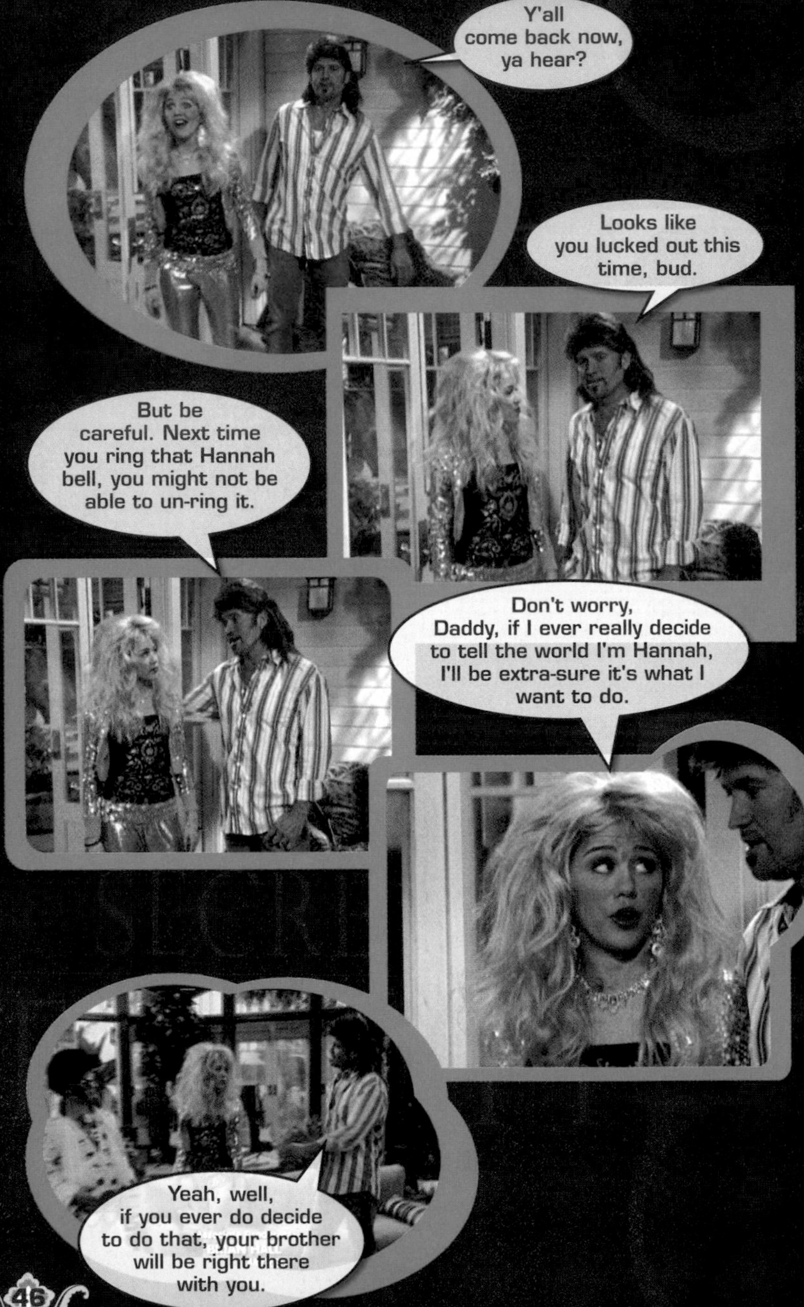
Y'all come back now, ya hear?
Looks like you lucked out this time, bud.
But be careful. Next time you ring that Hannah bell, you might not be able to un-ring it.
Don't worry, Daddy, if I ever really decide to tell the world I'm Hannah, I'll be extra-sure it's what I want to do.
Yeah, well, if you ever do decide to do that, your brother will be right there with you.

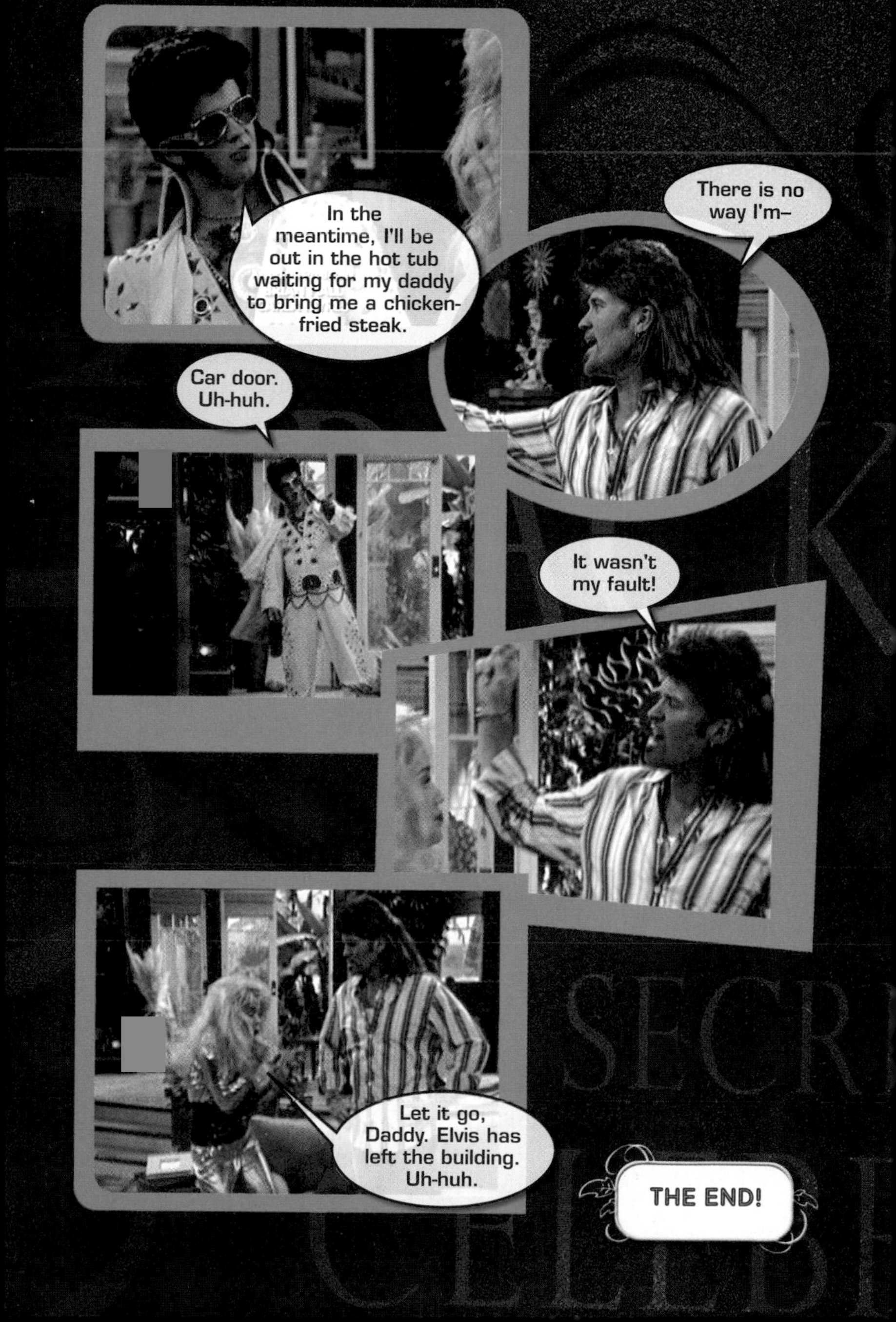
In the meantime, I'll be out in the hot tub waiting for my daddy to bring me a chicken-fried steak.
There is no way I'm–
Car door. Uh-huh.
It wasn't my fault!
Let it go, Daddy. Elvis has left the building. Uh-huh.
THE END!

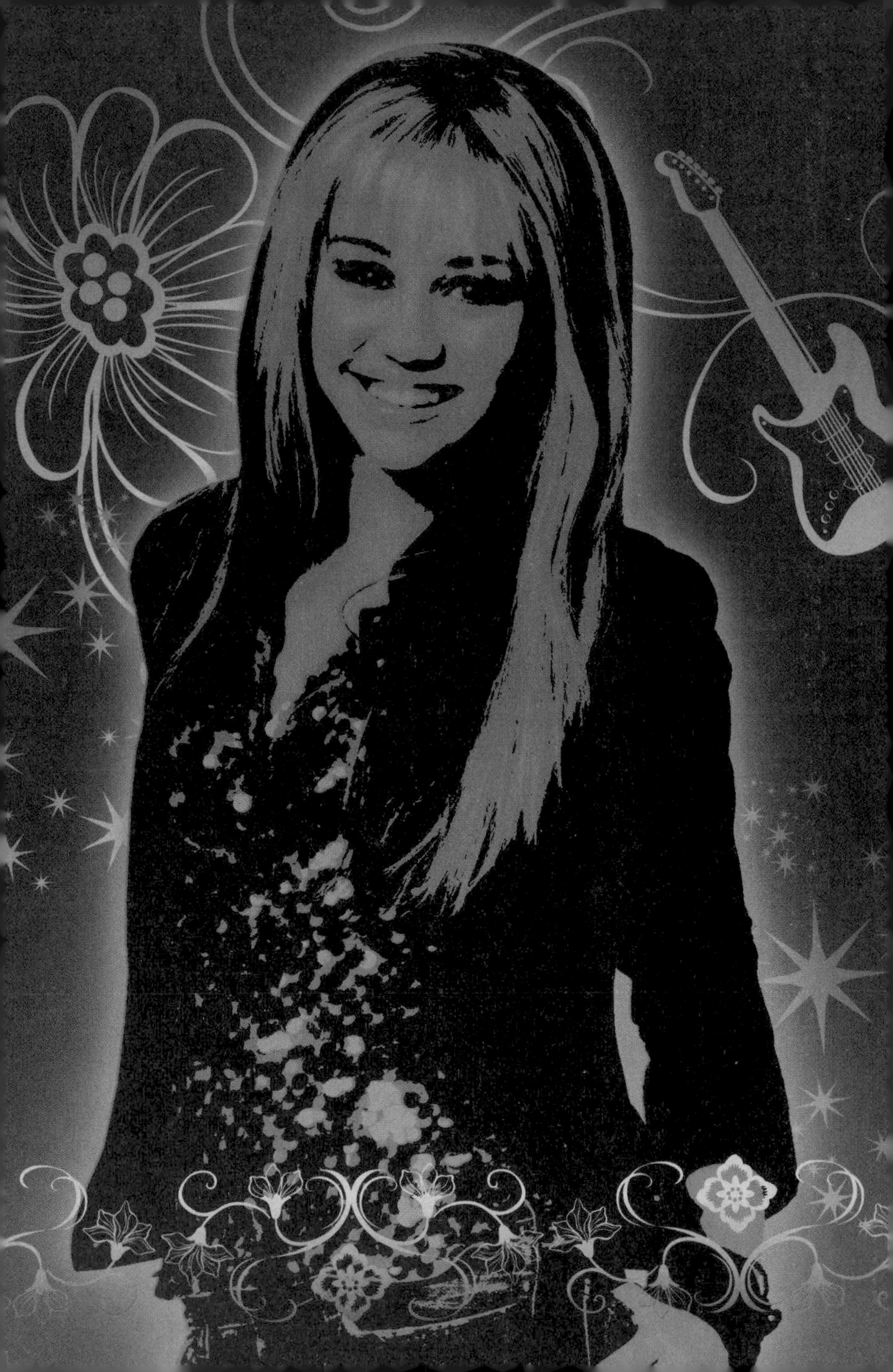

# "MORE THAN A ZOMBIE TO ME"

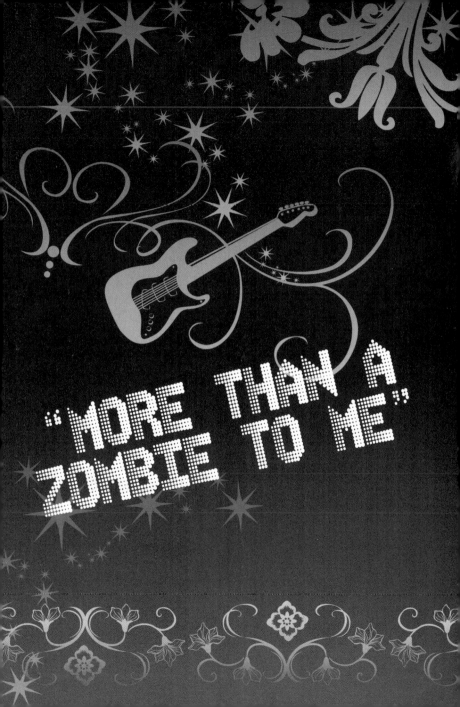

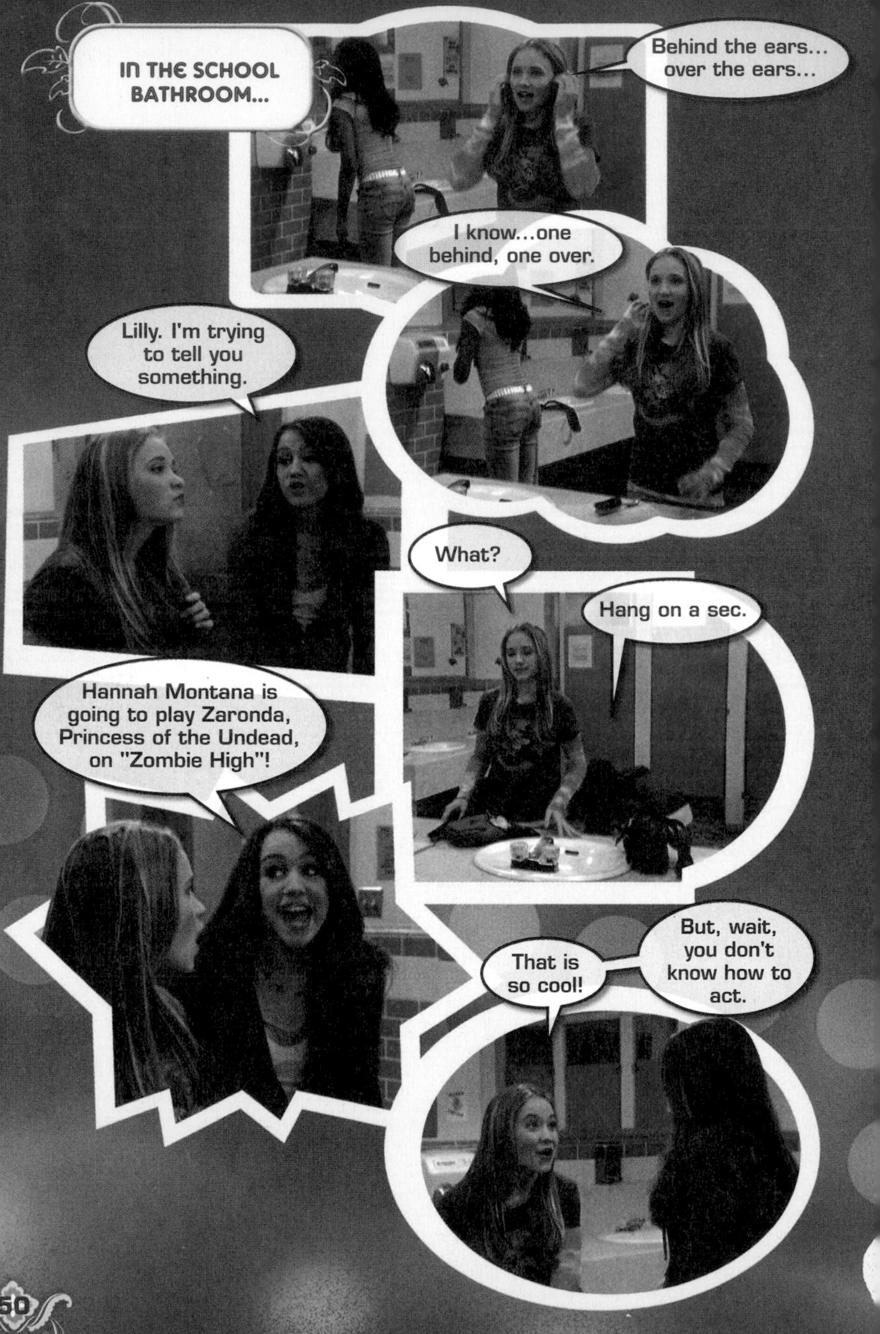
IN THE SCHOOL BATHROOM...
Behind the ears... over the ears...
I know...one behind, one over.
Lilly. I'm trying to tell you something.
What?
Hang on a sec.
Hannah Montana is going to play Zaronda, Princess of the Undead, on "Zombie High"!
That is so cool!
But, wait, you don't know how to act.

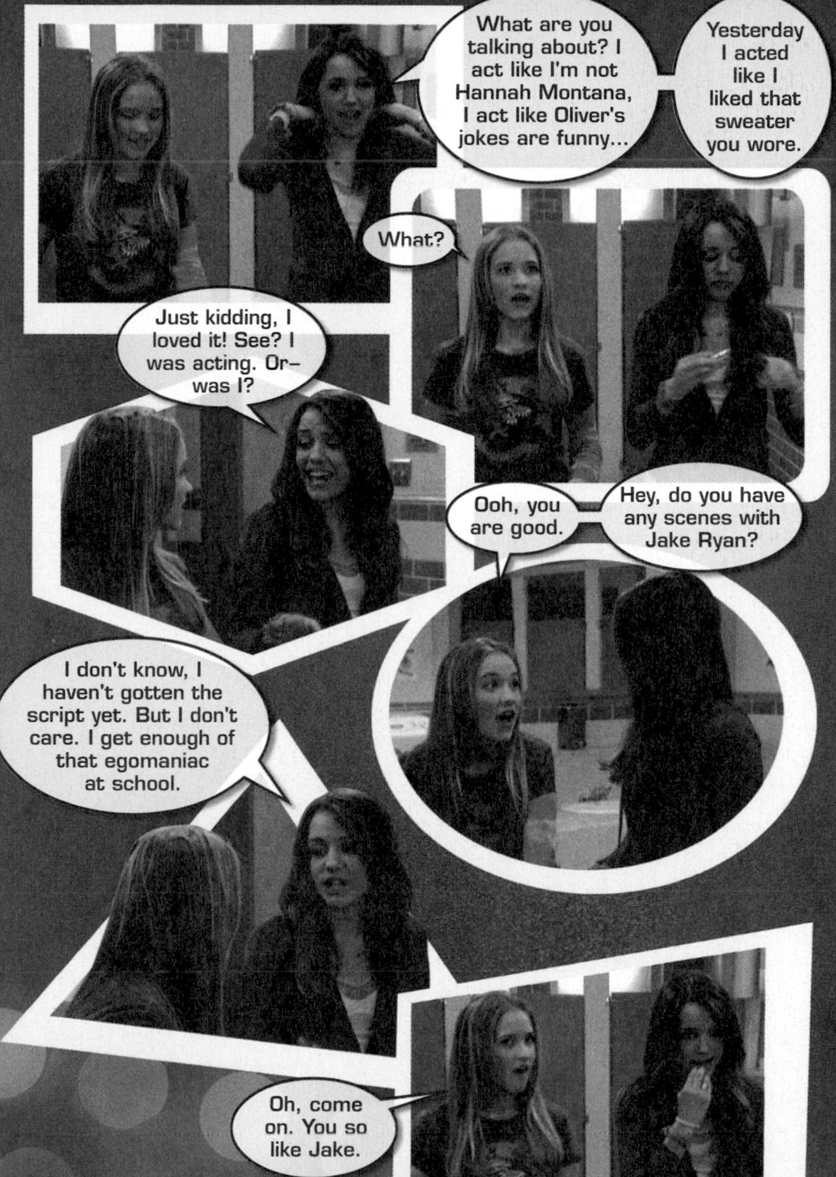
What are you talking about? I act like I'm not Hannah Montana, I act like Oliver's jokes are funny...
Yesterday I acted like I liked that sweater you wore.
What?
Just kidding, I loved it! See? I was acting. Or– was I?
Ooh, you are good.
Hey, do you have any scenes with Jake Ryan?
I don't know, I haven't gotten the script yet. But I don't care. I get enough of that egomaniac at school.
Oh, come on. You so like Jake.

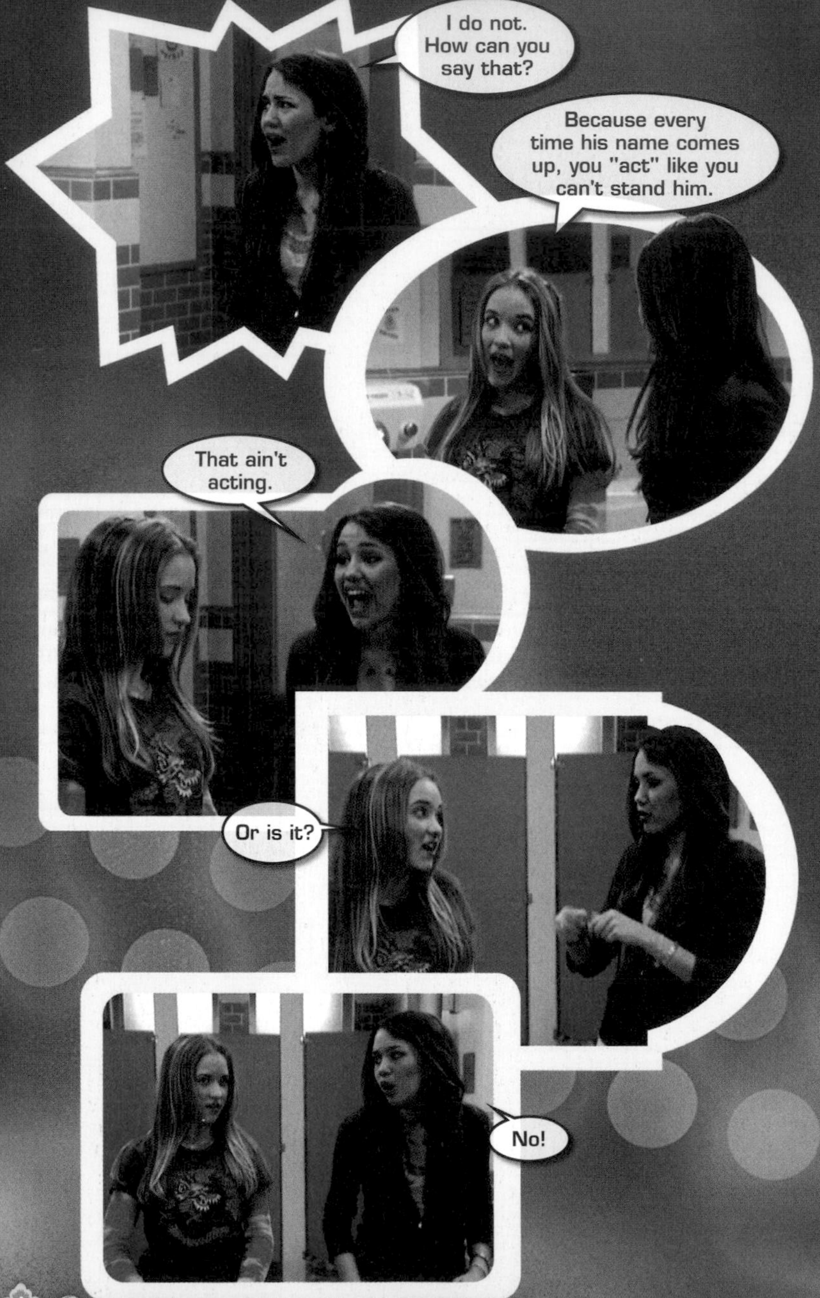
I do not. How can you say that?
Because every time his name comes up, you "act" like you can't stand him.
That ain't acting.
Or is it?
No!

LATER...
Hey, have you guys heard? Sometime today Jake's gonna ask one lucky girl to the '70s Dance.
As soon as he picks one, there'll be a hundred depressed girls lookin' for a shoulder to cry on. Here it is, broad and water absorbent.
Look at him, it's disgusting.
SIGH!
Oh, come on, if he asks you to the dance, are you telling me you wouldn't say "yes"?
Yes.
Yes, you'd say "no"? Or, yes, you'd say "yes"?

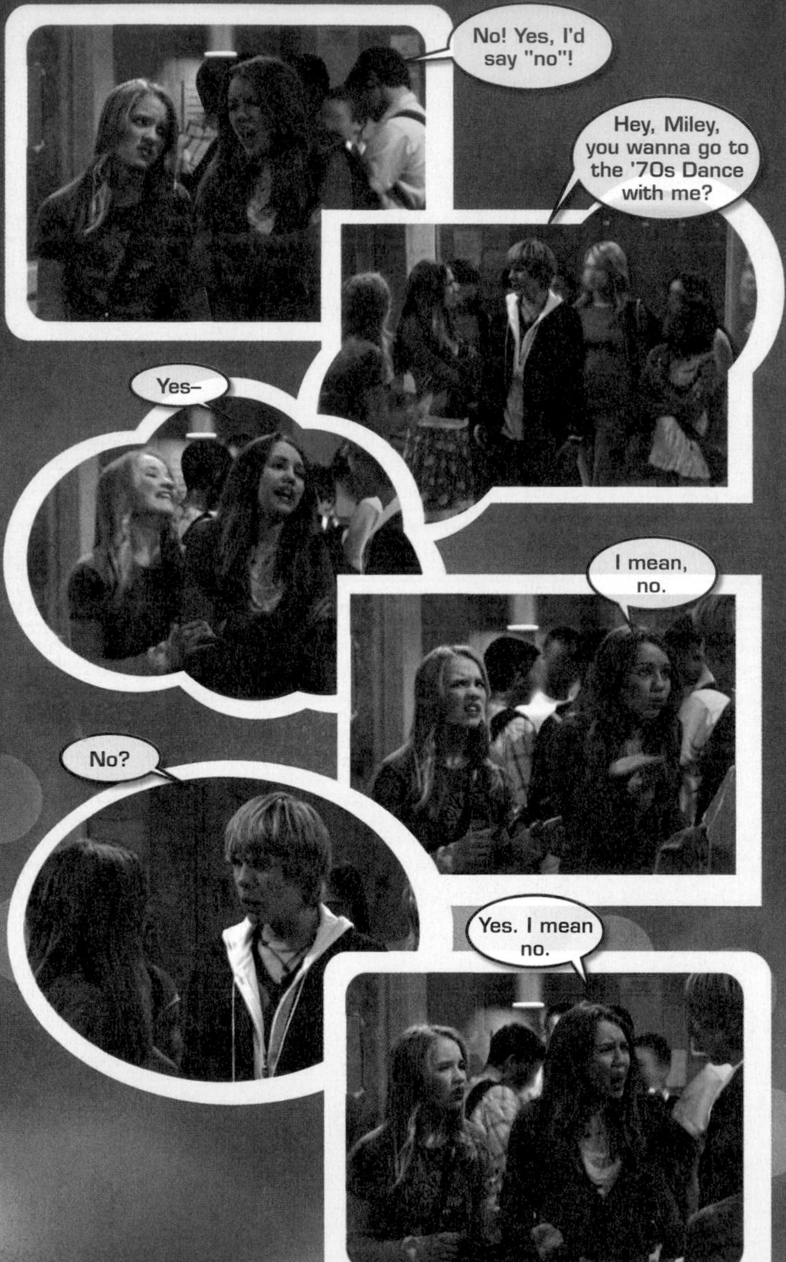
No! Yes, I'd say "no"!
Hey, Miley, you wanna go to the '70s Dance with me?
Yes–
I mean, no.
No?
Yes. I mean no.

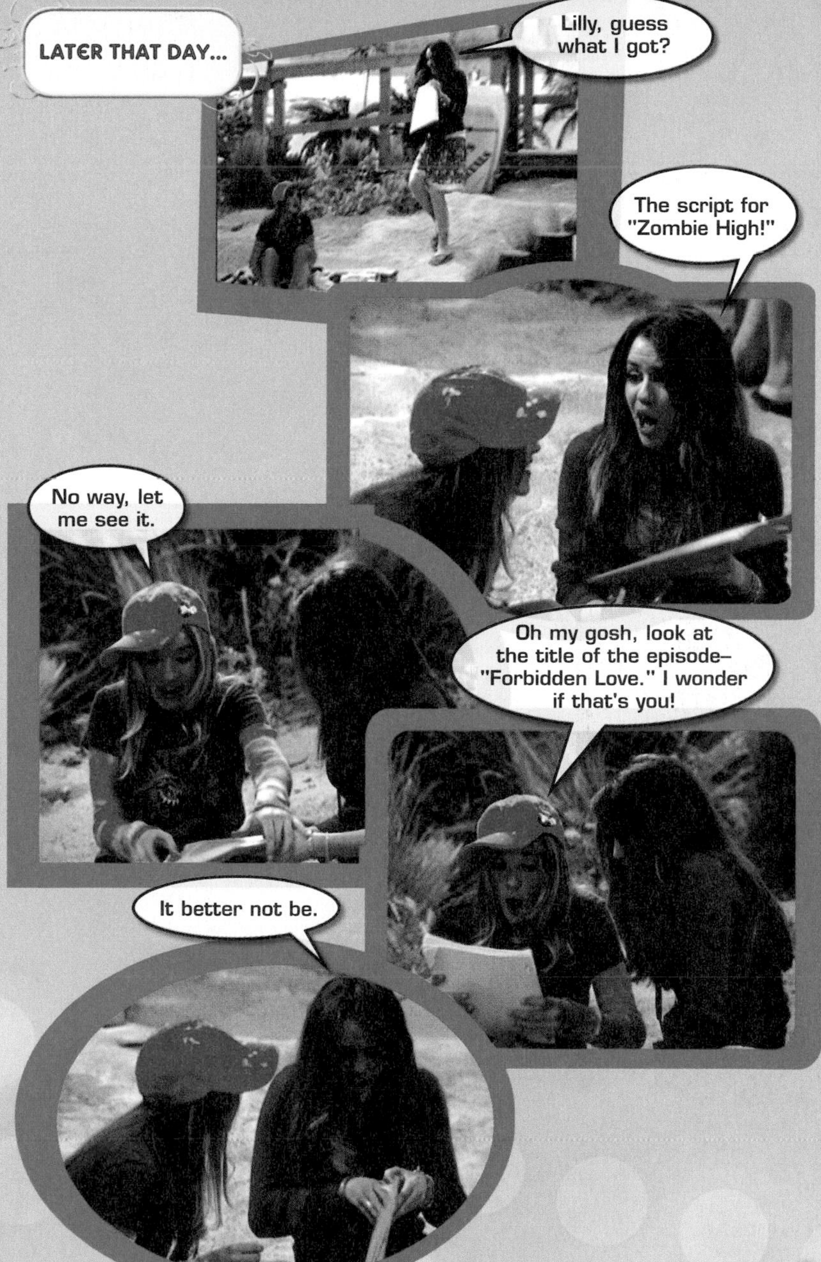
LATER THAT DAY...
Lilly, guess what I got?
The script for "Zombie High!"
No way, let me see it.
Oh my gosh, look at the title of the episode– "Forbidden Love." I wonder if that's you!
It better not be.

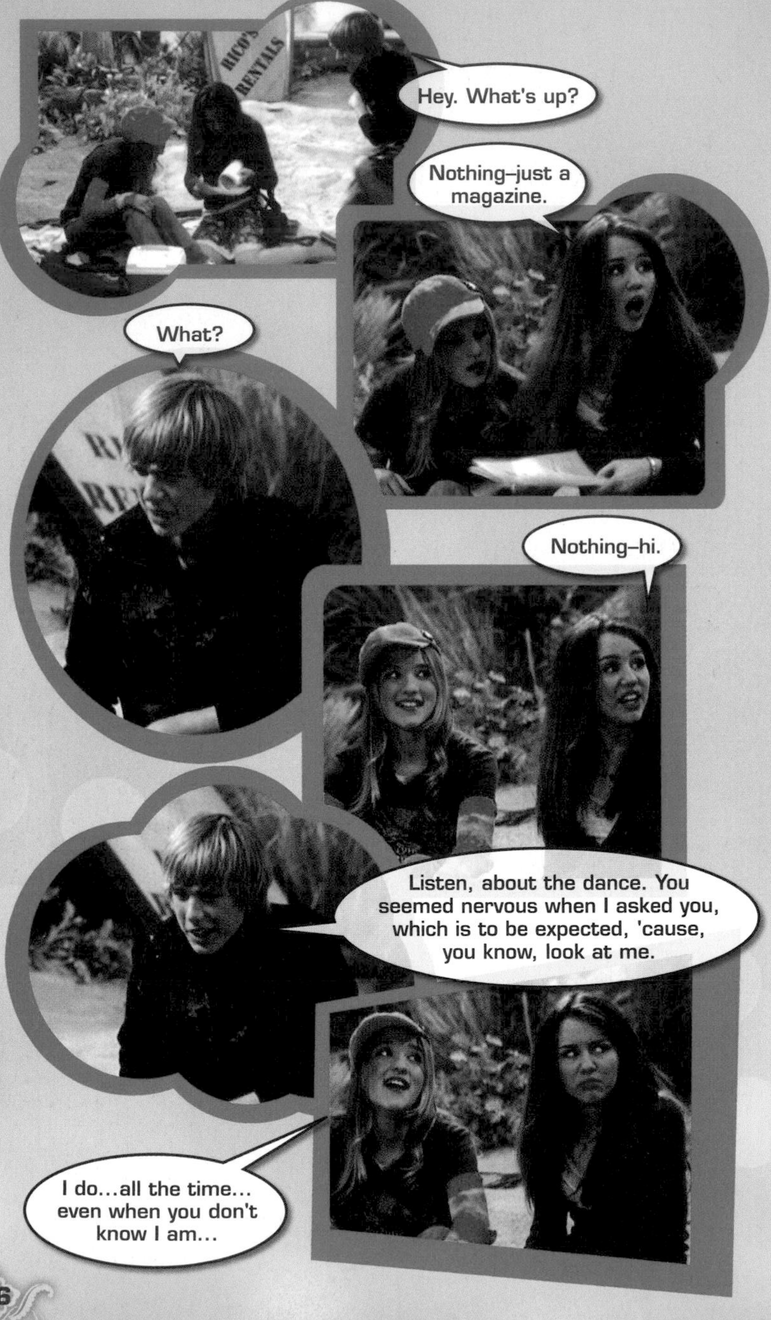

Hey. What's up?
Nothing–just a magazine.
What?
Nothing–hi.
Listen, about the dance. You seemed nervous when I asked you, which is to be expected, 'cause, you know, look at me.
I do...all the time... even when you don't know I am...

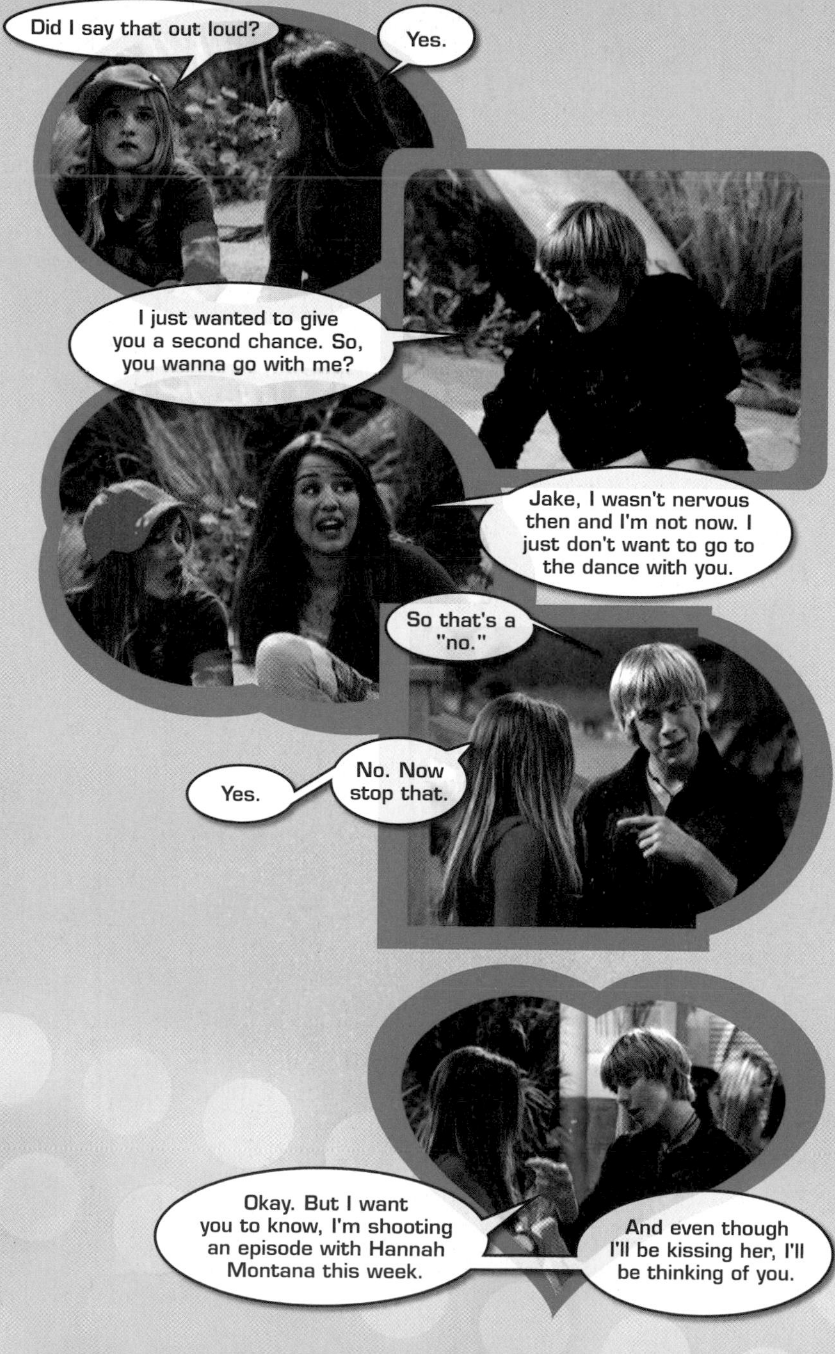

Did I say that out loud?
Yes.
I just wanted to give you a second chance. So, you wanna go with me?
Jake, I wasn't nervous then and I'm not now. I just don't want to go to the dance with you.
So that's a "no."
Yes.
No. Now stop that.
Okay. But I want you to know, I'm shooting an episode with Hannah Montana this week.
And even though I'll be kissing her, I'll be thinking of you.

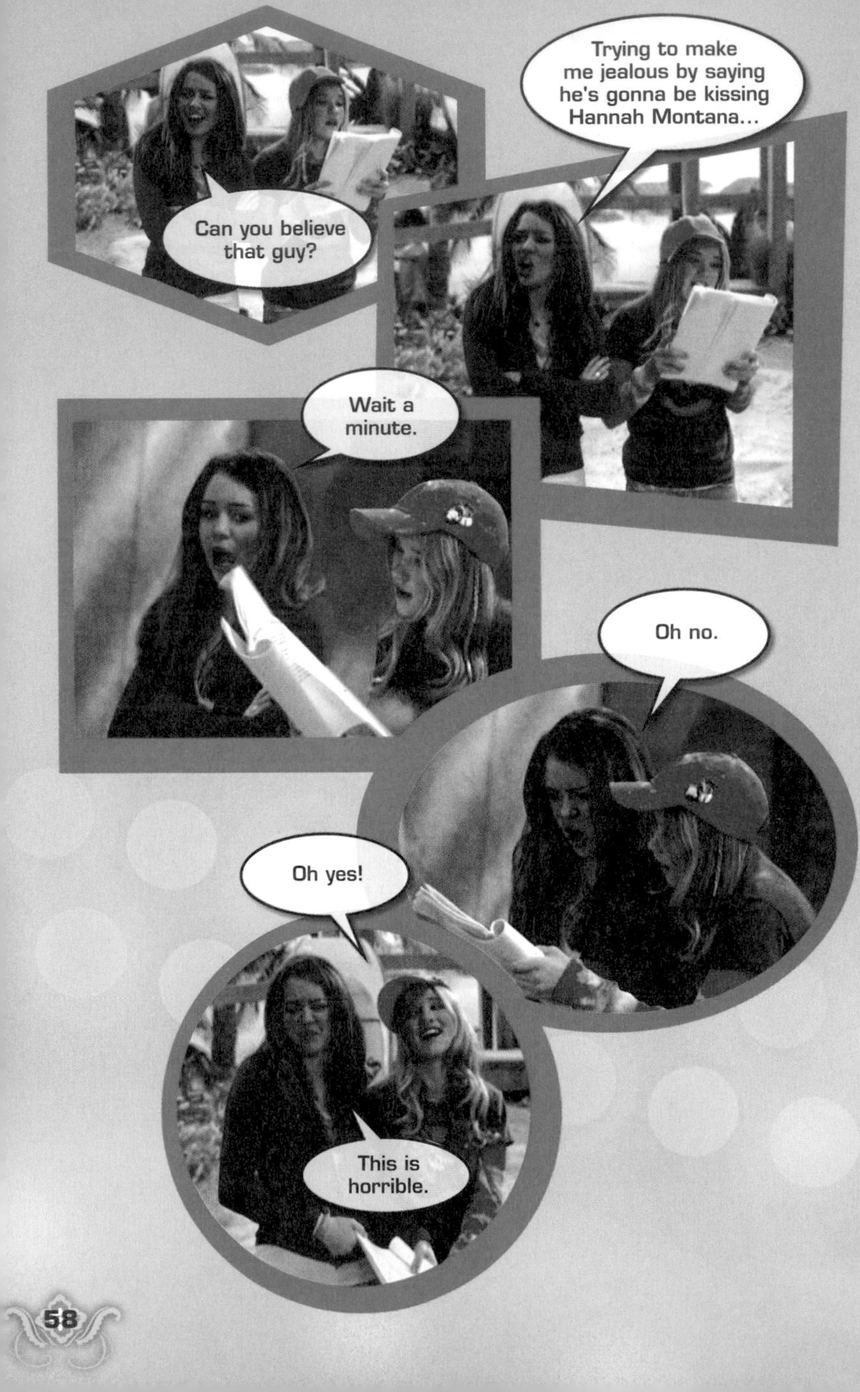
Can you believe that guy?
Trying to make me jealous by saying he's gonna be kissing Hannah Montana...
Wait a minute.
Oh no.
Oh yes!
This is horrible.

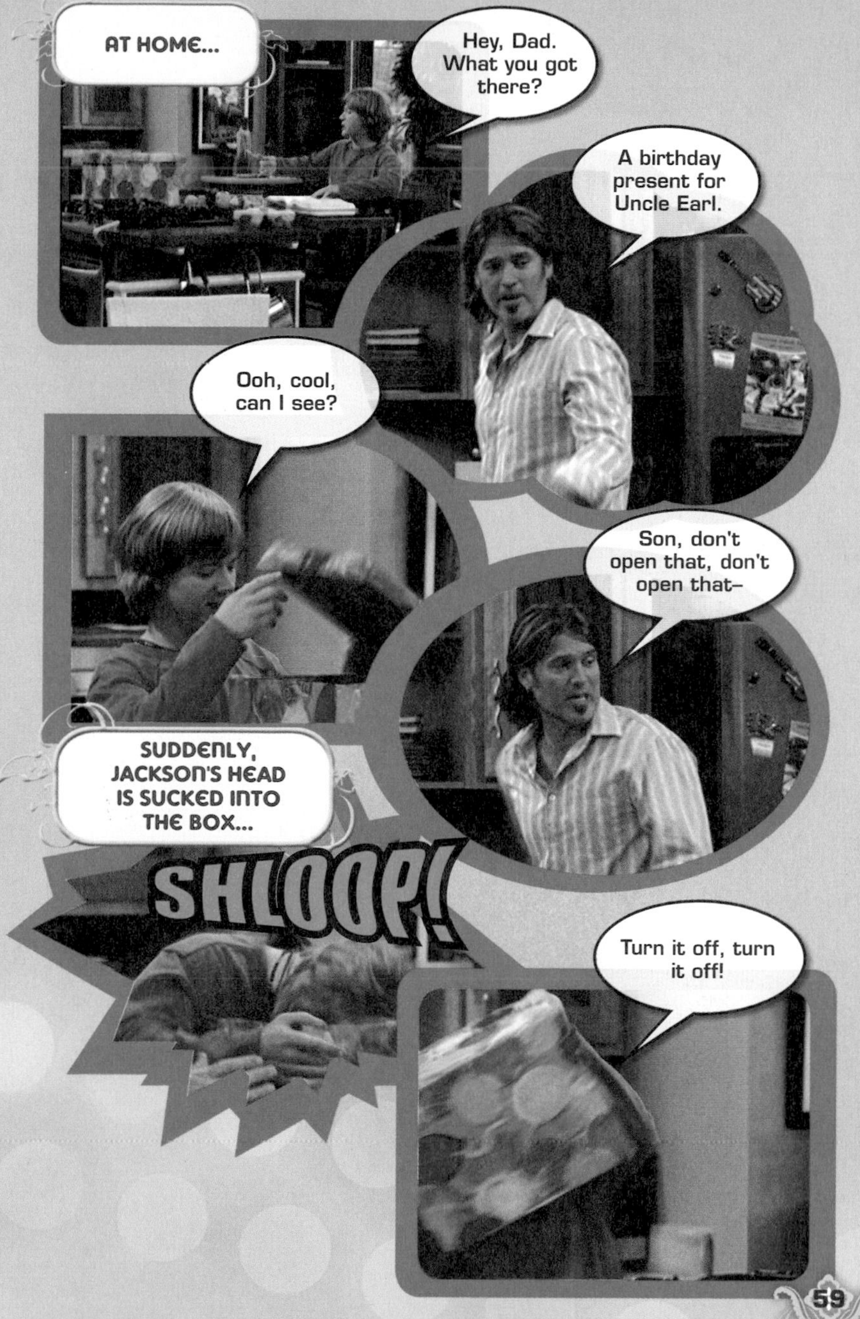
AT HOME...
Hey, Dad. What you got there?
A birthday present for Uncle Earl.
Ooh, cool, can I see?
Son, don't open that, don't open that–
SUDDENLY, JACKSON'S HEAD IS SUCKED INTO THE BOX...
SHLOOP!
Turn it off, turn it off!

FINALLY, JACKSON MANAGES TO WRESTLE THE BOX OFF...

What is wrong with you?

I'm sorry, son. I told you not to open it.

You know how Uncle Earl always sends me a prank for my birthday?

Well, this year I decided it was time for a vacuum-packed payback.

Ooh, can I get in on it?

Jackson, no offense, but this game's for the big boys. I wouldn't want you to get hurt.

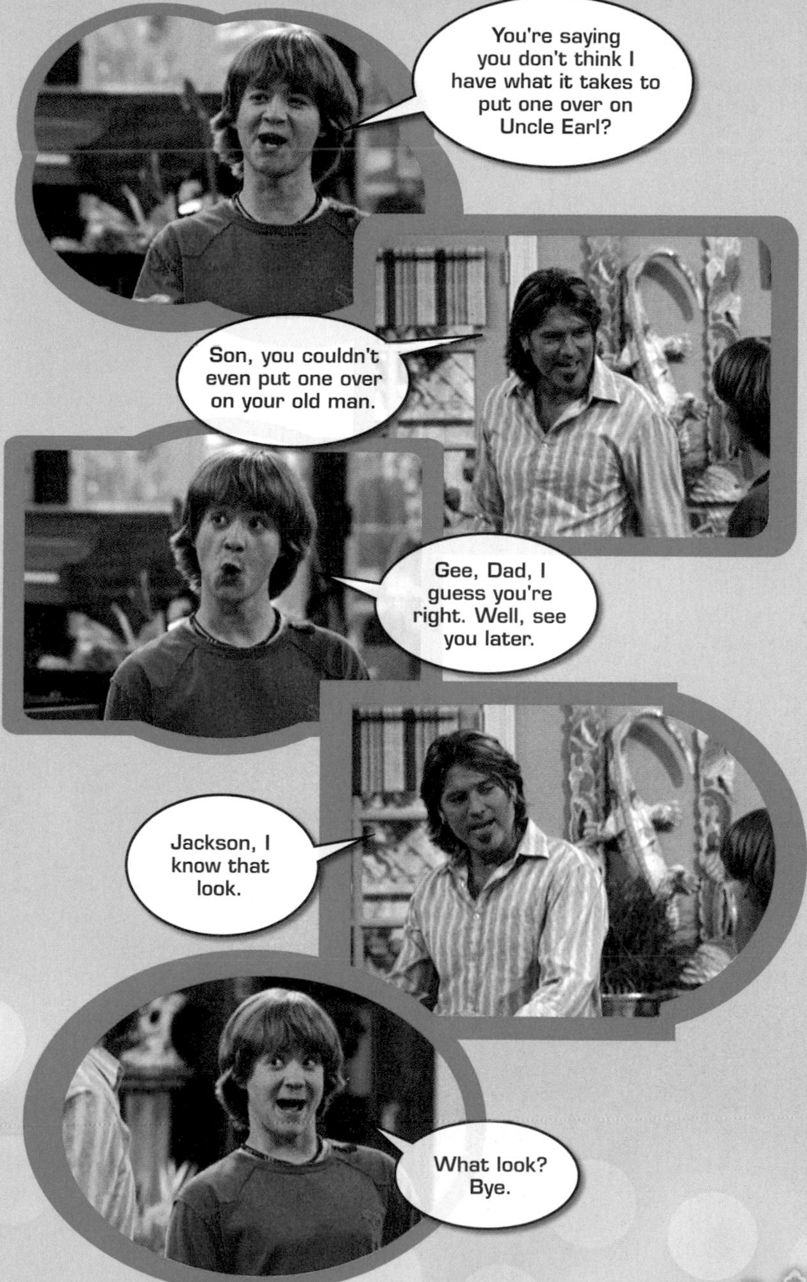
You're saying you don't think I have what it takes to put one over on Uncle Earl?
Son, you couldn't even put one over on your old man.
Gee, Dad, I guess you're right. Well, see you later.
Jackson, I know that look.
What look? Bye.

Hi, Hannah, I'm Roger, your director. Big fan, big fan.
You look horrible. It's fantastic!
Listen, I've been thinking about the script... Do I really have to kiss that zombie slayer?
I mean, can't his faithful sidekick Demon Dog save the world this week? I'd rather plant one on the pooch.
Interesting idea. I'll mention it to the writers.
But for now, just try to have fun. And remember, all of us here...big fans, big fans.

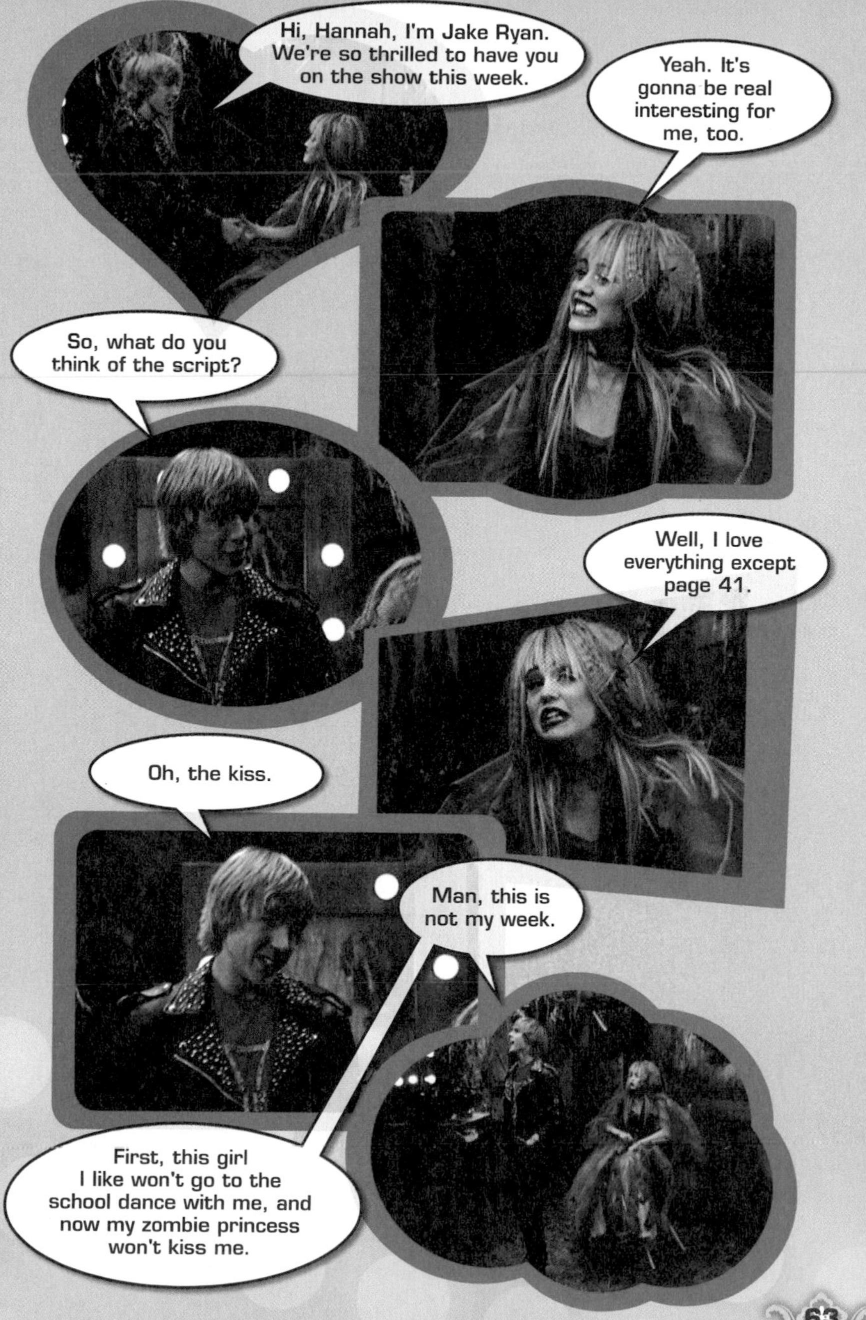
Hi, Hannah, I'm Jake Ryan. We're so thrilled to have you on the show this week.
Yeah. It's gonna be real interesting for me, too.
So, what do you think of the script?
Well, I love everything except page 41.
Oh, the kiss.
Man, this is not my week.
First, this girl I like won't go to the school dance with me, and now my zombie princess won't kiss me.

Yeah, well, I just don't think the zombie princess...
Who's this girl at school?
Her name's Miley.
Wow. What an interesting name. I've never heard anything like it. She must be really unique.
She is. She's cute and funny and smart–she's so down-to-earth.
When I talk to her, I feel like she's not talking to Jake Ryan the celebrity–she's talking to Jake Ryan the guy. You know?
Yeah, I do. Sometimes you need to know people like you for you and not just because you're a star.

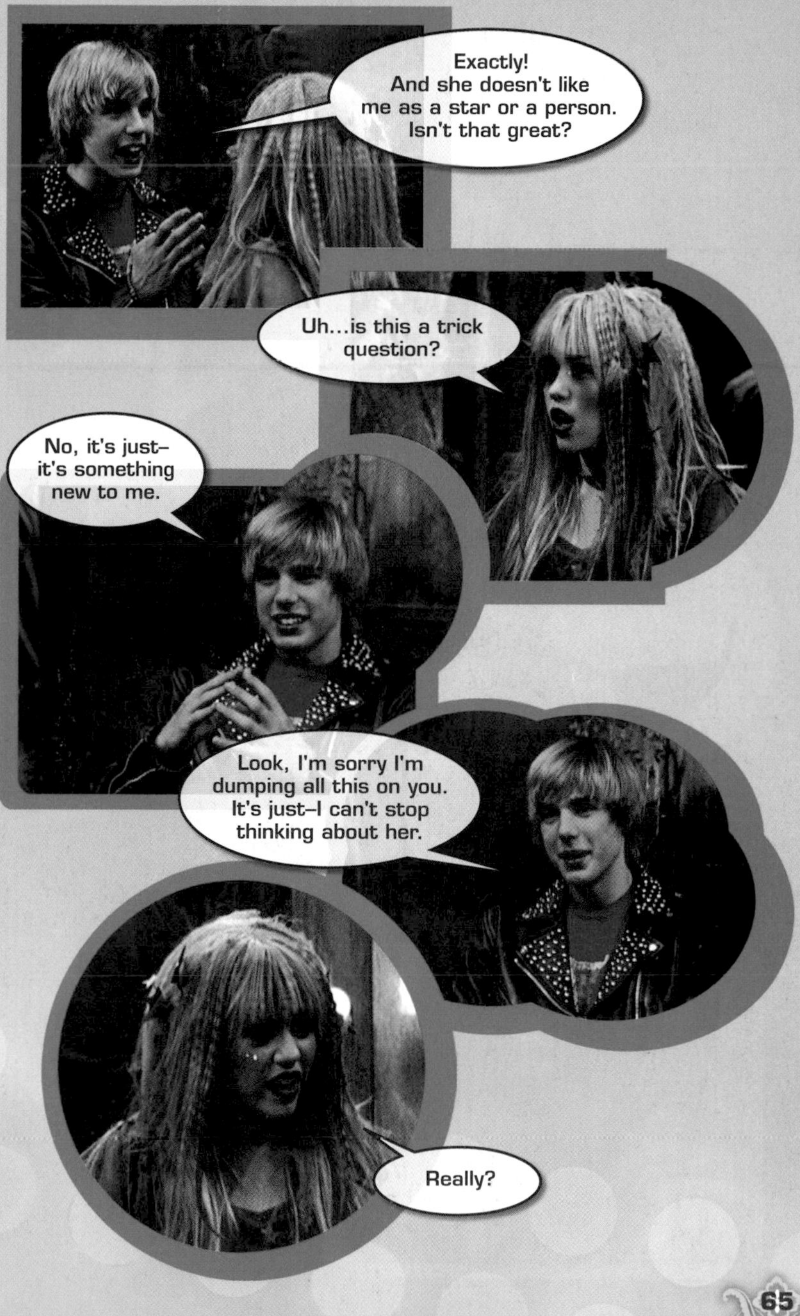
Exactly! And she doesn't like me as a star or a person. Isn't that great?
Uh...is this a trick question?
No, it's just– it's something new to me.
Look, I'm sorry I'm dumping all this on you. It's just–I can't stop thinking about her.
Really?

Well, I guess I'm just gonna have to forget about it.
Uh, yeah, right, I suppose forgetting about her's good.
So, uh, back to this kiss. Just close your eyes and count to 60. It'll be over before you know it.
Sixty?!
SSST!
Hope you like Thunder Mint.

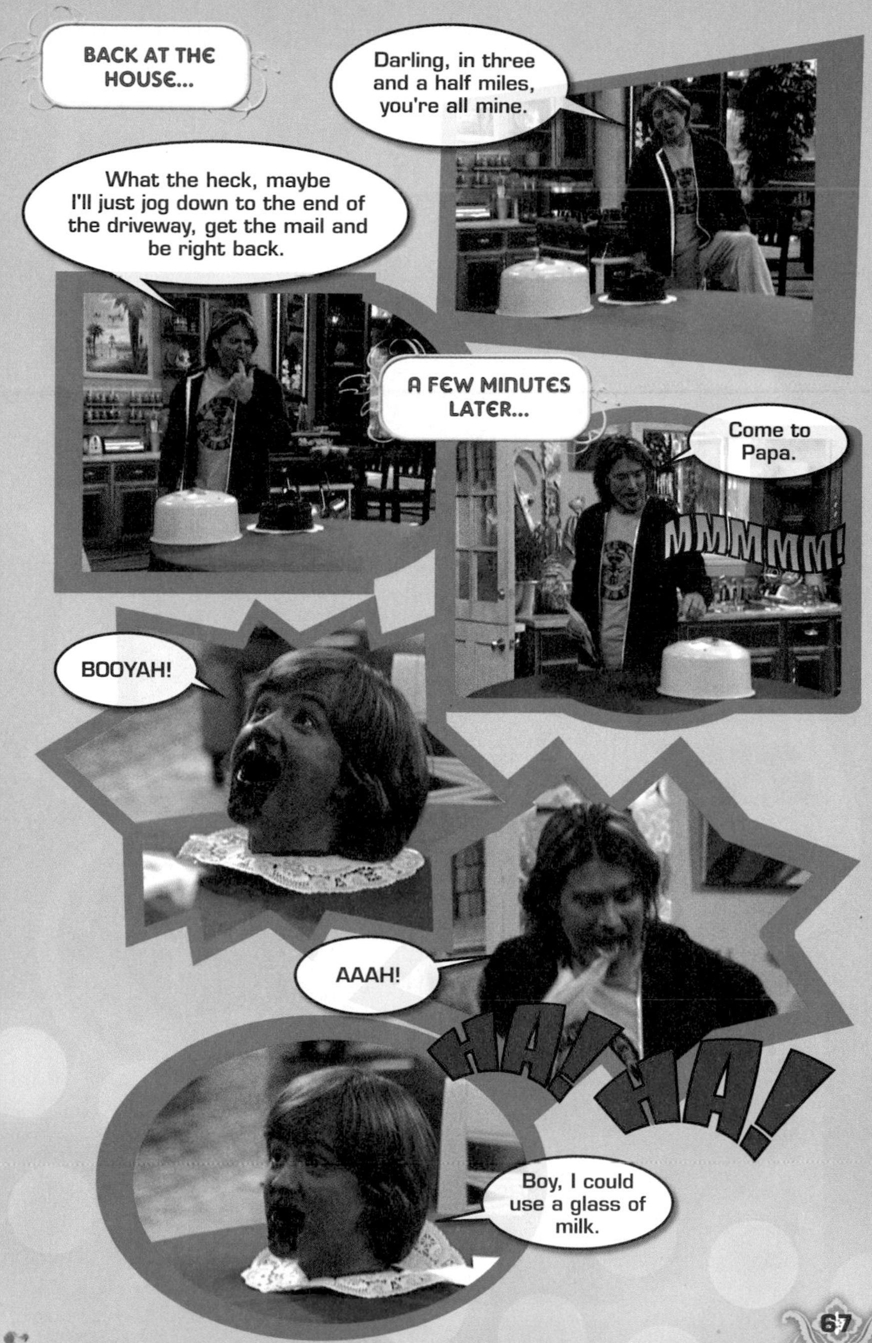
BACK AT THE HOUSE...
Darling, in three and a half miles, you're all mine.
What the heck, maybe I'll just jog down to the end of the driveway, get the mail and be right back.
A FEW MINUTES LATER...
Come to Papa.
MMMMMM!
BOOYAH!
AAAH!
HA! HA!
Boy, I could use a glass of milk.

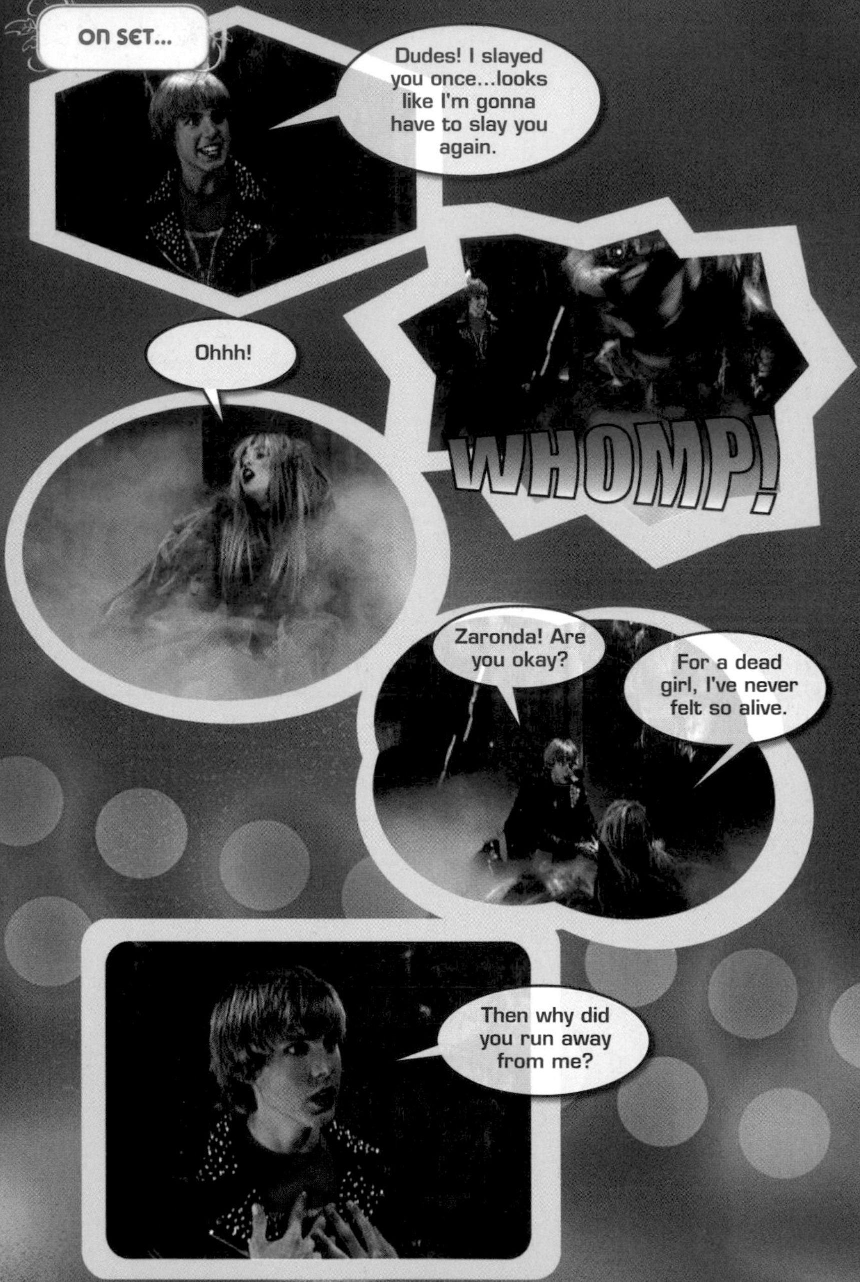
ON SET...
Dudes! I slayed you once...looks like I'm gonna have to slay you again.
WHOMP!
Ohhh!
Zaronda! Are you okay?
For a dead girl, I've never felt so alive.
Then why did you run away from me?

Don't you see? Our love is forbidden. We can never be together.
Then maybe this will change your mind.
He really is cute. And he thinks I'm cute...and down to earth.
Oh, stop it, Miley, you don't like him...
Oh, who am I kidding? Yes, I do. And that Thunder Mint...wow!
PUCKER!
CUT!

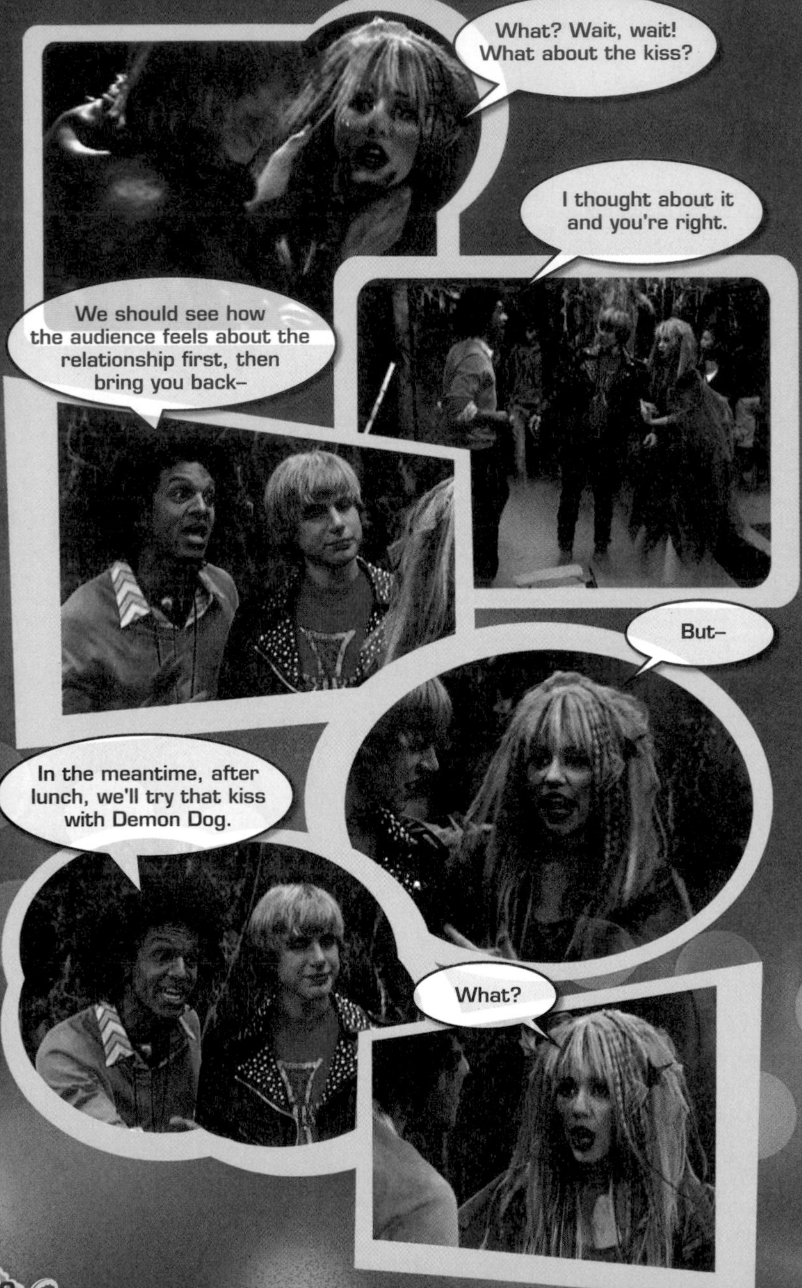
What? Wait, wait! What about the kiss?
I thought about it and you're right.
We should see how the audience feels about the relationship first, then bring you back–
But–
In the meantime, after lunch, we'll try that kiss with Demon Dog.
What?

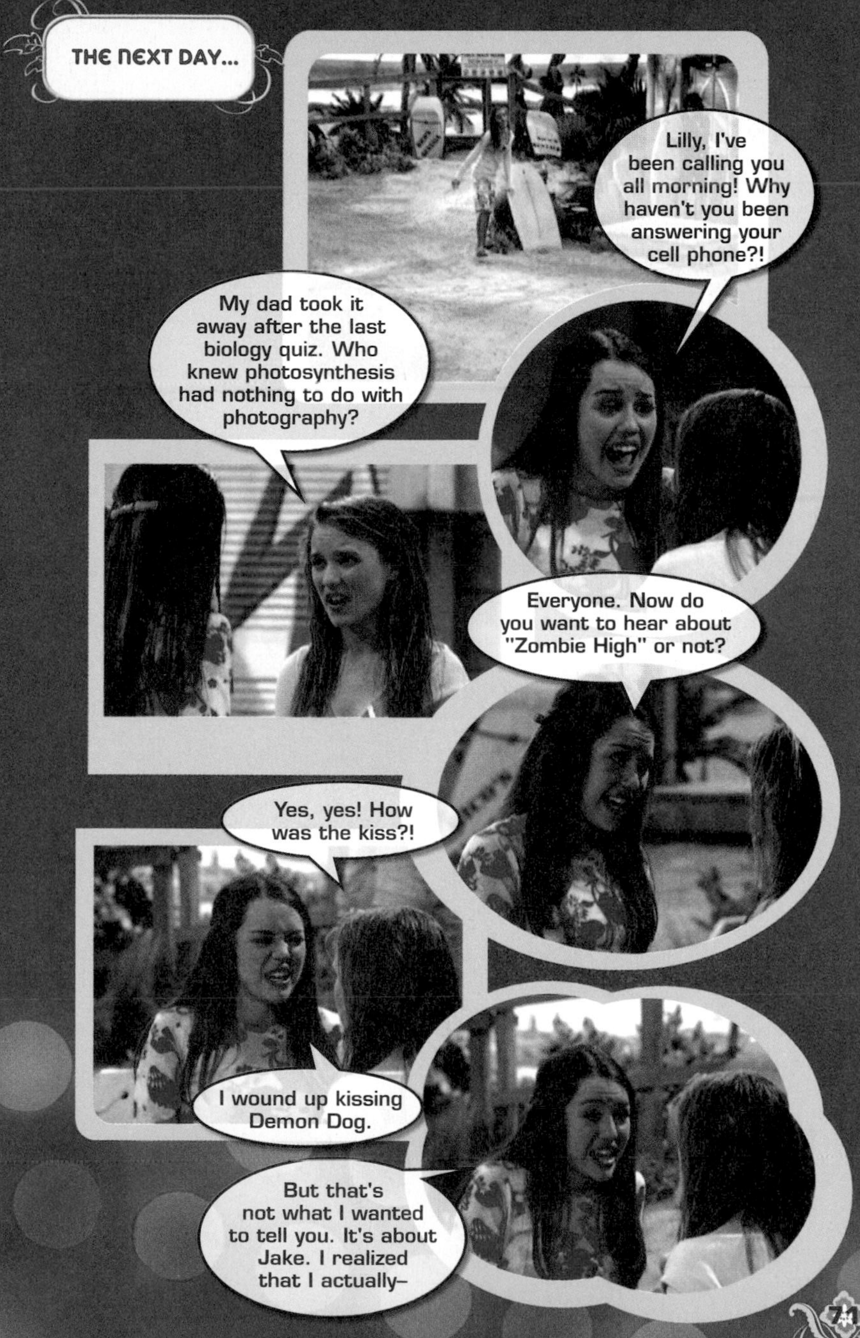
THE NEXT DAY...
Lilly, I've been calling you all morning! Why haven't you been answering your cell phone?!
My dad took it away after the last biology quiz. Who knew photosynthesis had nothing to do with photography?
Everyone. Now do you want to hear about "Zombie High" or not?
Yes, yes! How was the kiss?!
I wound up kissing Demon Dog.
But that's not what I wanted to tell you. It's about Jake. I realized that I actually–

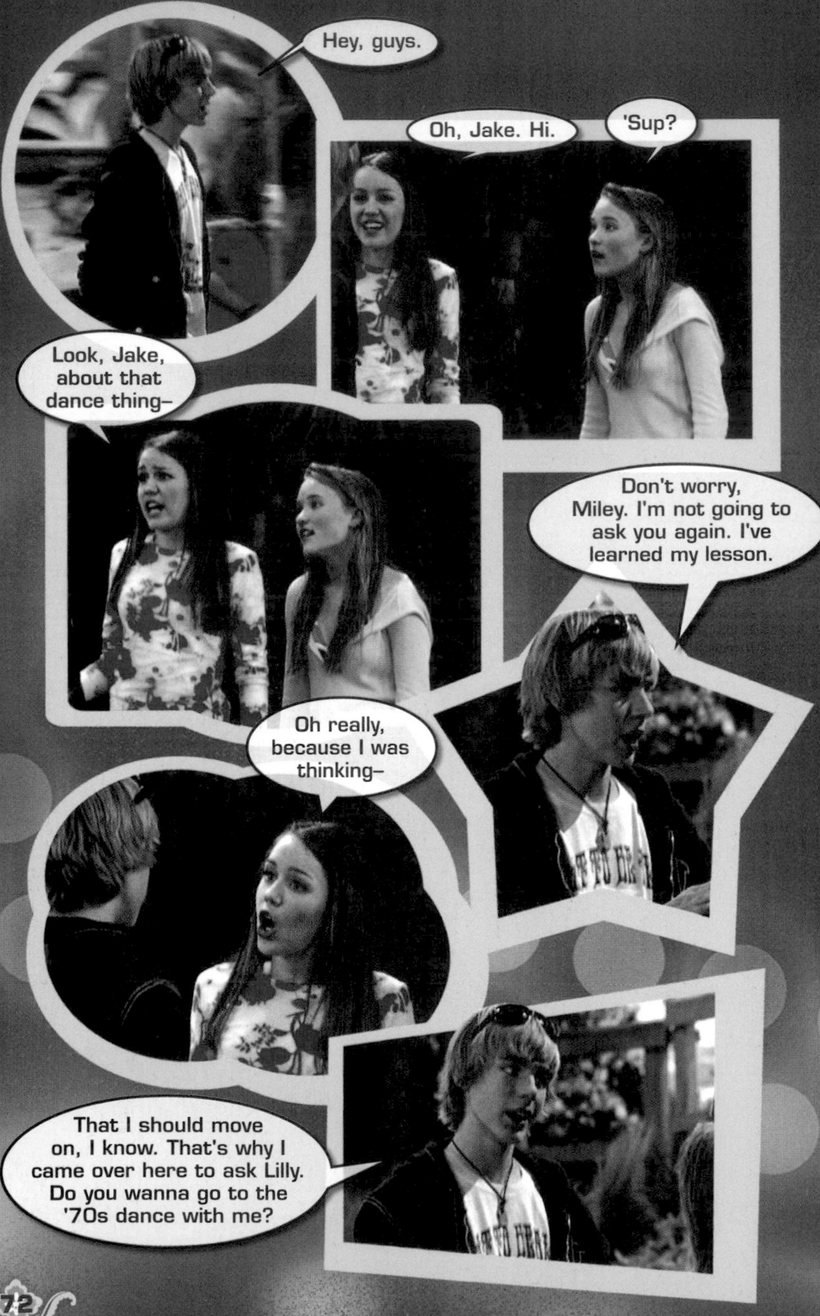
Hey, guys.
Oh, Jake. Hi.
'Sup?
Look, Jake, about that dance thing–
Don't worry, Miley. I'm not going to ask you again. I've learned my lesson.
Oh really, because I was thinking–
That I should move on, I know. That's why I came over here to ask Lilly. Do you wanna go to the '70s dance with me?

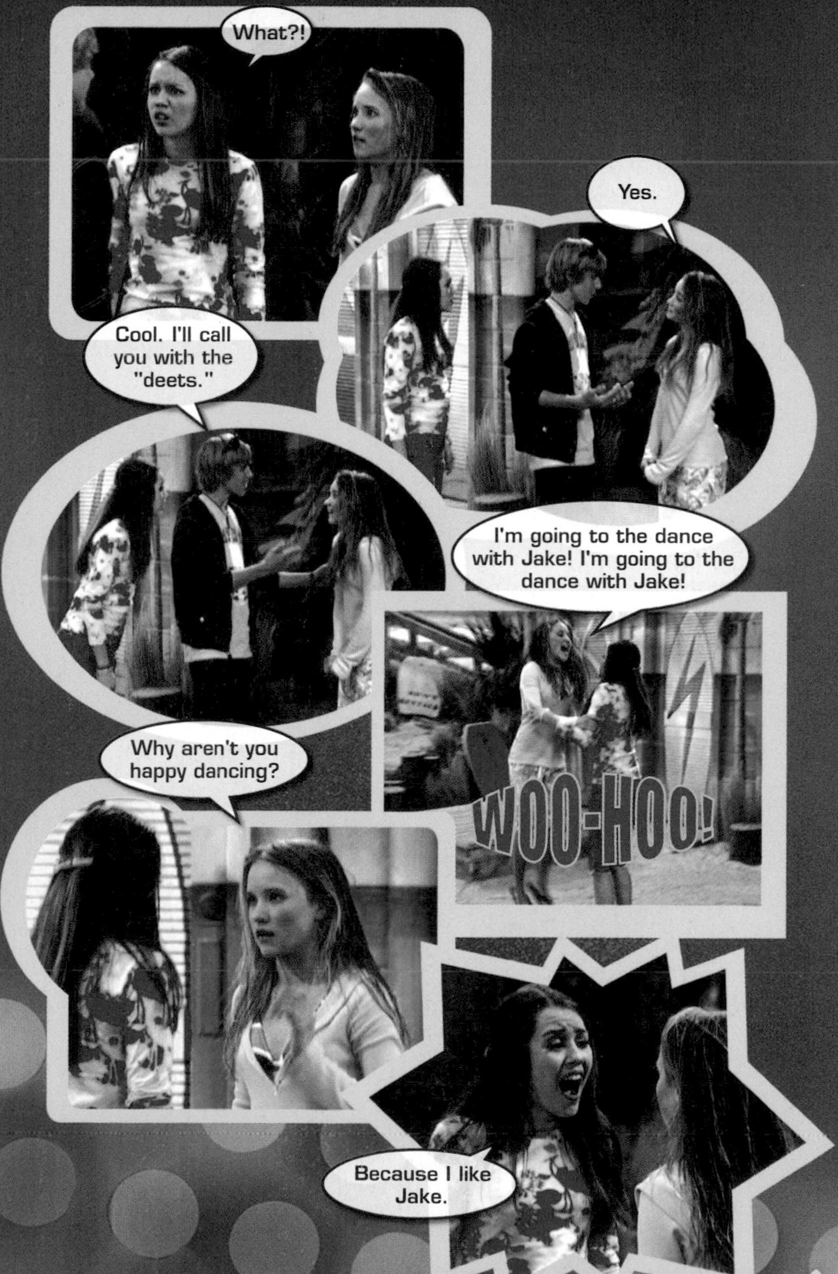
What?!
Yes.
Cool. I'll call you with the "deets."
I'm going to the dance with Jake! I'm going to the dance with Jake!
WOO-HOO!
Why aren't you happy dancing?
Because I like Jake.

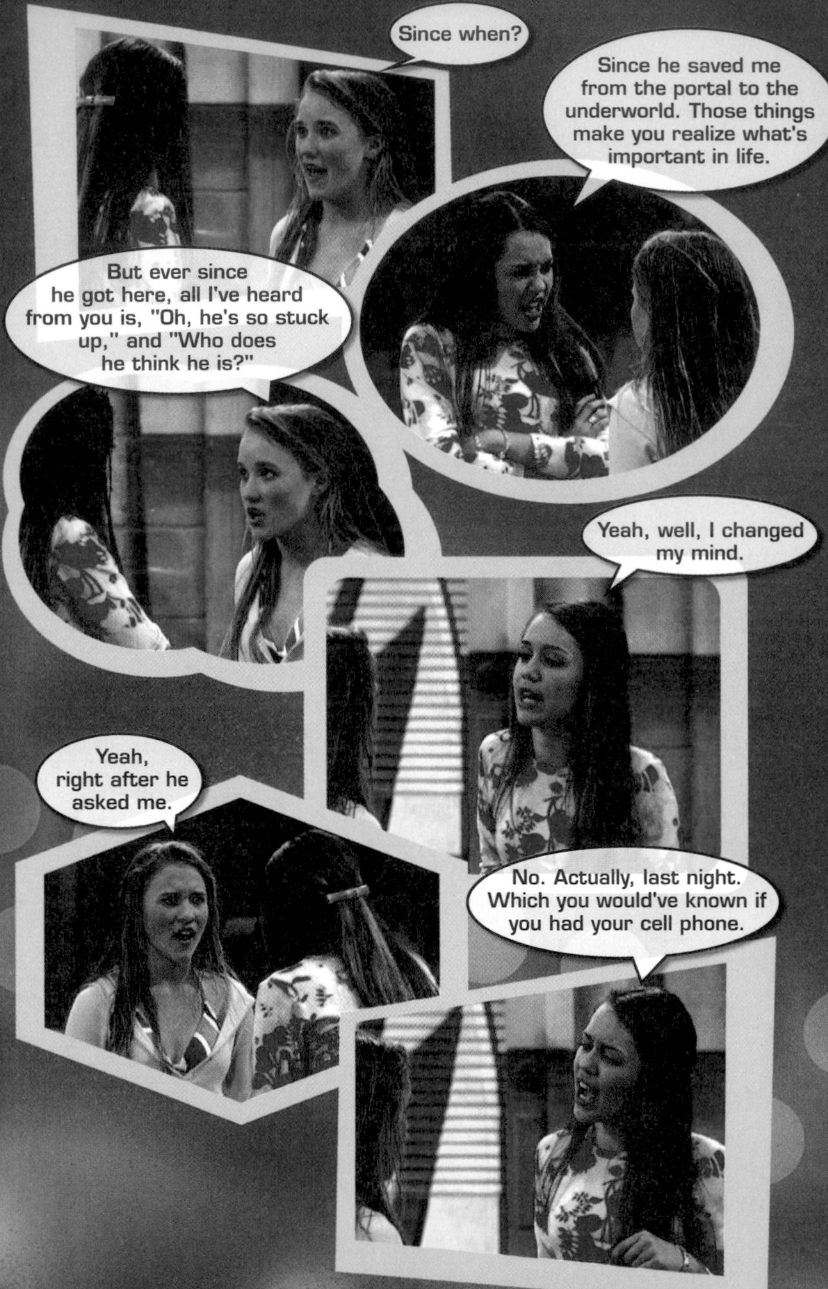
Since when?
Since he saved me from the portal to the underworld. Those things make you realize what's important in life.
But ever since he got here, all I've heard from you is, "Oh, he's so stuck up," and "Who does he think he is?"
Yeah, well, I changed my mind.
Yeah, right after he asked me.
No. Actually, last night. Which you would've known if you had your cell phone.

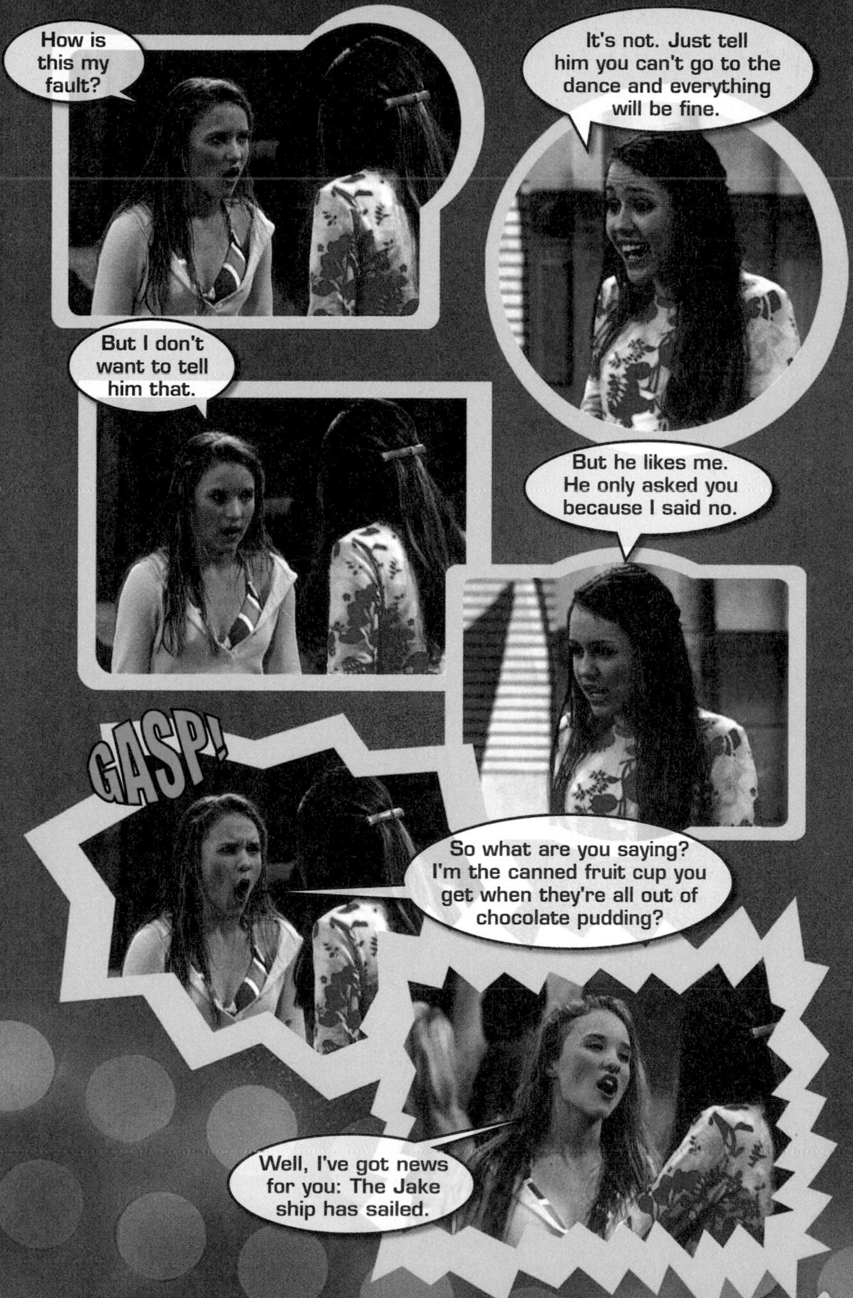
How is this my fault?
It's not. Just tell him you can't go to the dance and everything will be fine.
But I don't want to tell him that.
But he likes me. He only asked you because I said no.
GASP!
So what are you saying? I'm the canned fruit cup you get when they're all out of chocolate pudding?
Well, I've got news for you: The Jake ship has sailed.

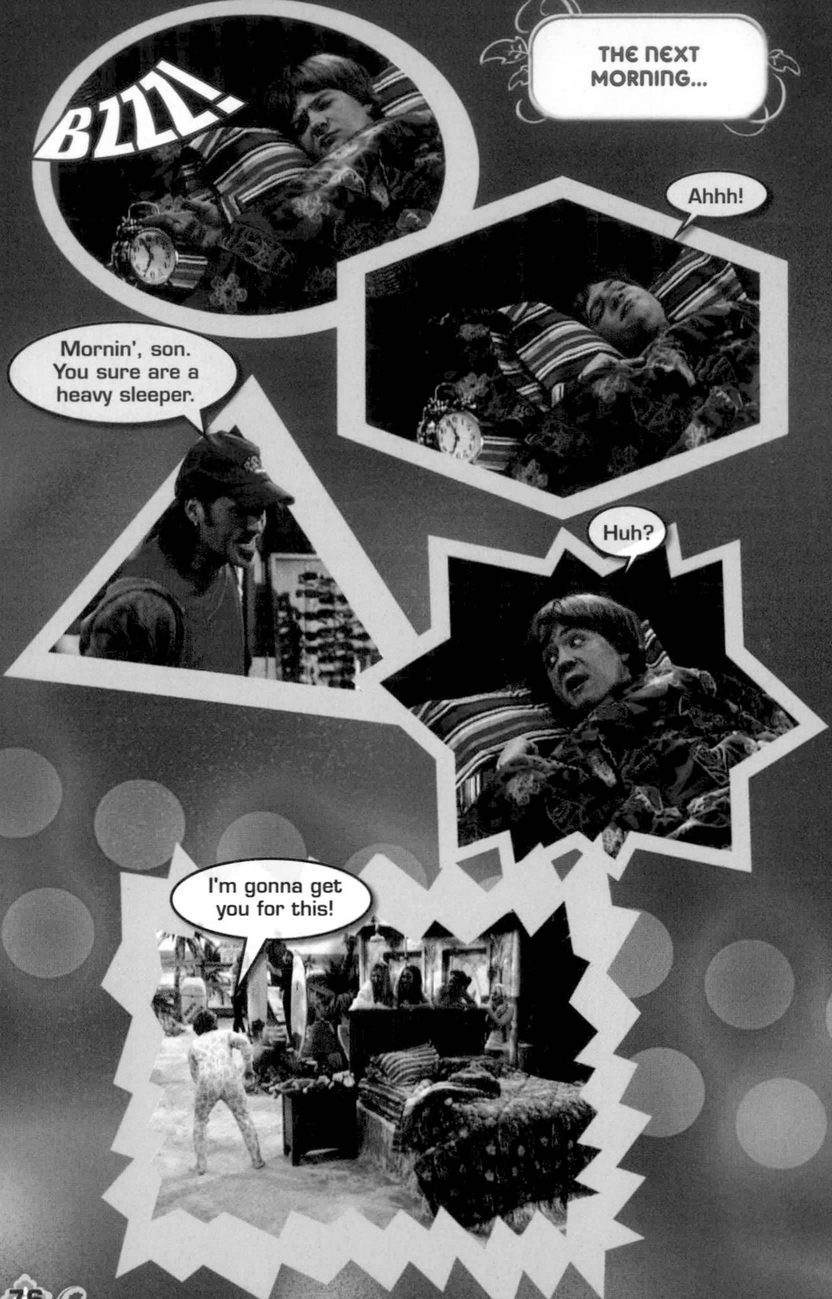
BZZZ!
THE NEXT MORNING...
Ahhh!
Mornin', son. You sure are a heavy sleeper.
Huh?
I'm gonna get you for this!

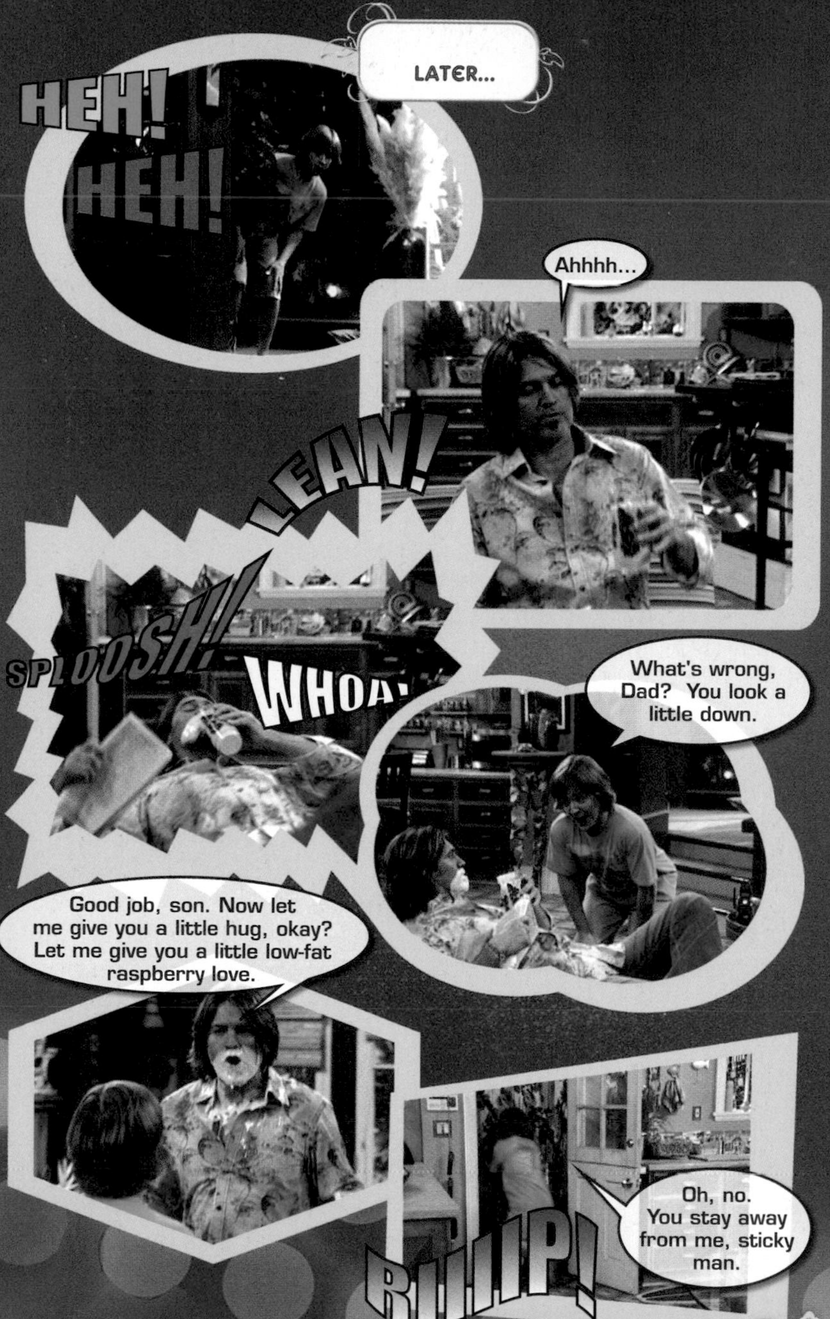
LATER...
HEH! HEH!
Ahhhh...
LEAN!
SPLOOSH!!
WHOA!
What's wrong, Dad? You look a little down.
Good job, son. Now let me give you a little hug, okay? Let me give you a little low-fat raspberry love.
RIIIP!
Oh, no. You stay away from me, sticky man.

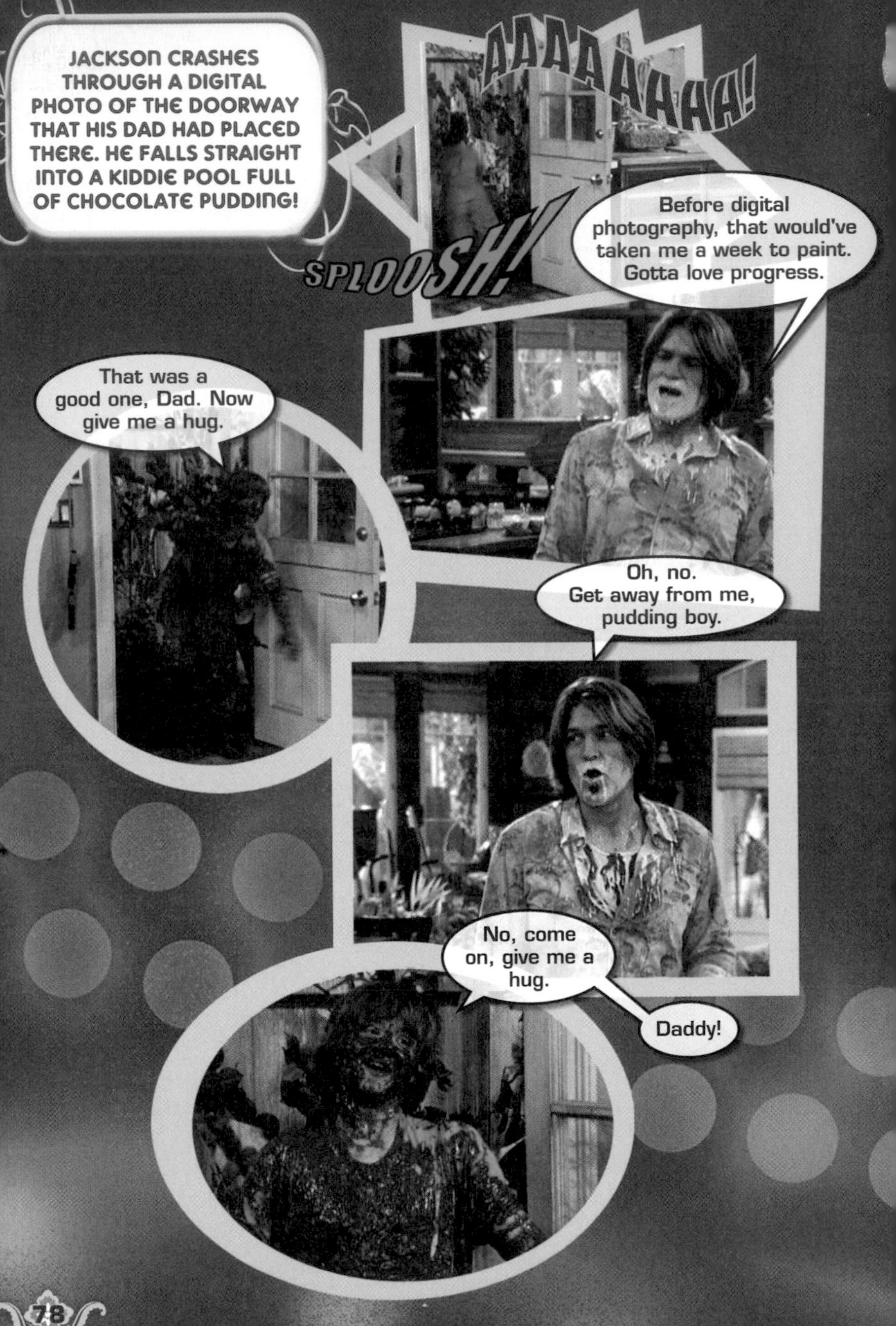
JACKSON CRASHES THROUGH A DIGITAL PHOTO OF THE DOORWAY THAT HIS DAD HAD PLACED THERE. HE FALLS STRAIGHT INTO A KIDDIE POOL FULL OF CHOCOLATE PUDDING!
AAAAAAAAH!
SPLOOSH!
Before digital photography, that would've taken me a week to paint. Gotta love progress.
That was a good one, Dad. Now give me a hug.
Oh, no. Get away from me, pudding boy.
No, come on, give me a hug.
Daddy!

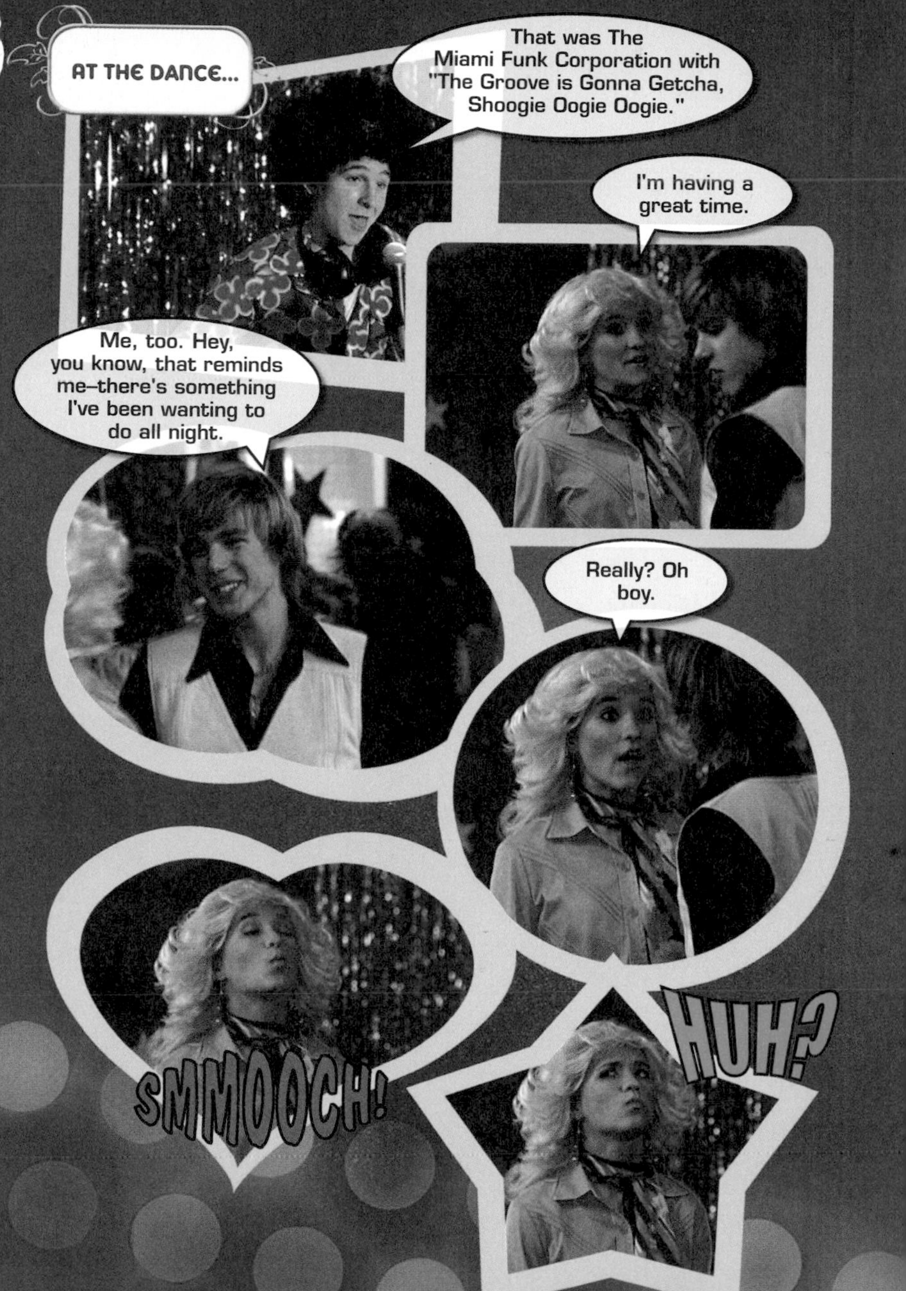
AT THE DANCE...
That was The Miami Funk Corporation with "The Groove is Gonna Getcha, Shoogie Oogie Oogie."
I'm having a great time.
Me, too. Hey, you know, that reminds me–there's something I've been wanting to do all night.
Really? Oh boy.
SMMOOCH!
HUH?

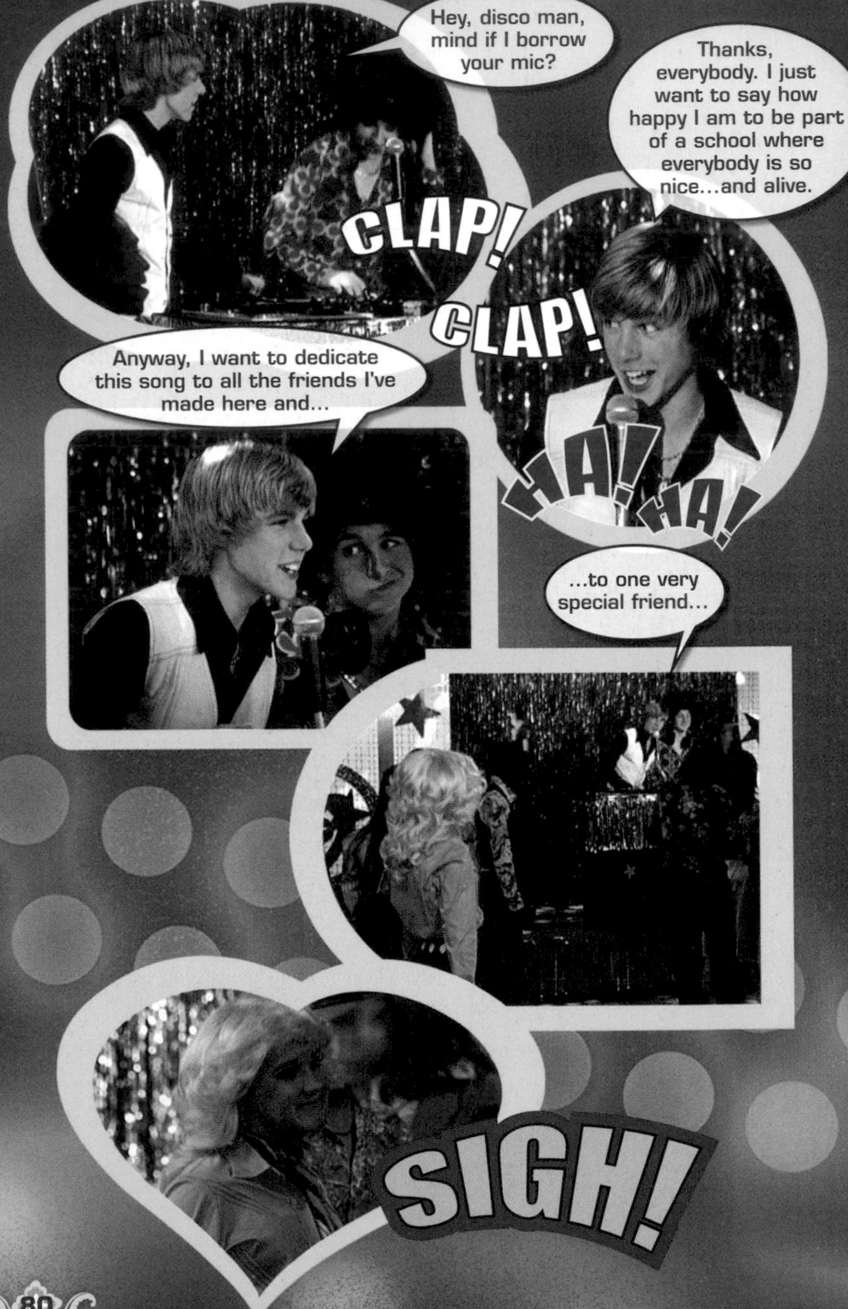

Hey, disco man, mind if I borrow your mic?
CLAP!
CLAP!
Thanks, everybody. I just want to say how happy I am to be part of a school where everybody is so nice...and alive.
HA! HA!
Anyway, I want to dedicate this song to all the friends I've made here and...
...to one very special friend...
SIGH!

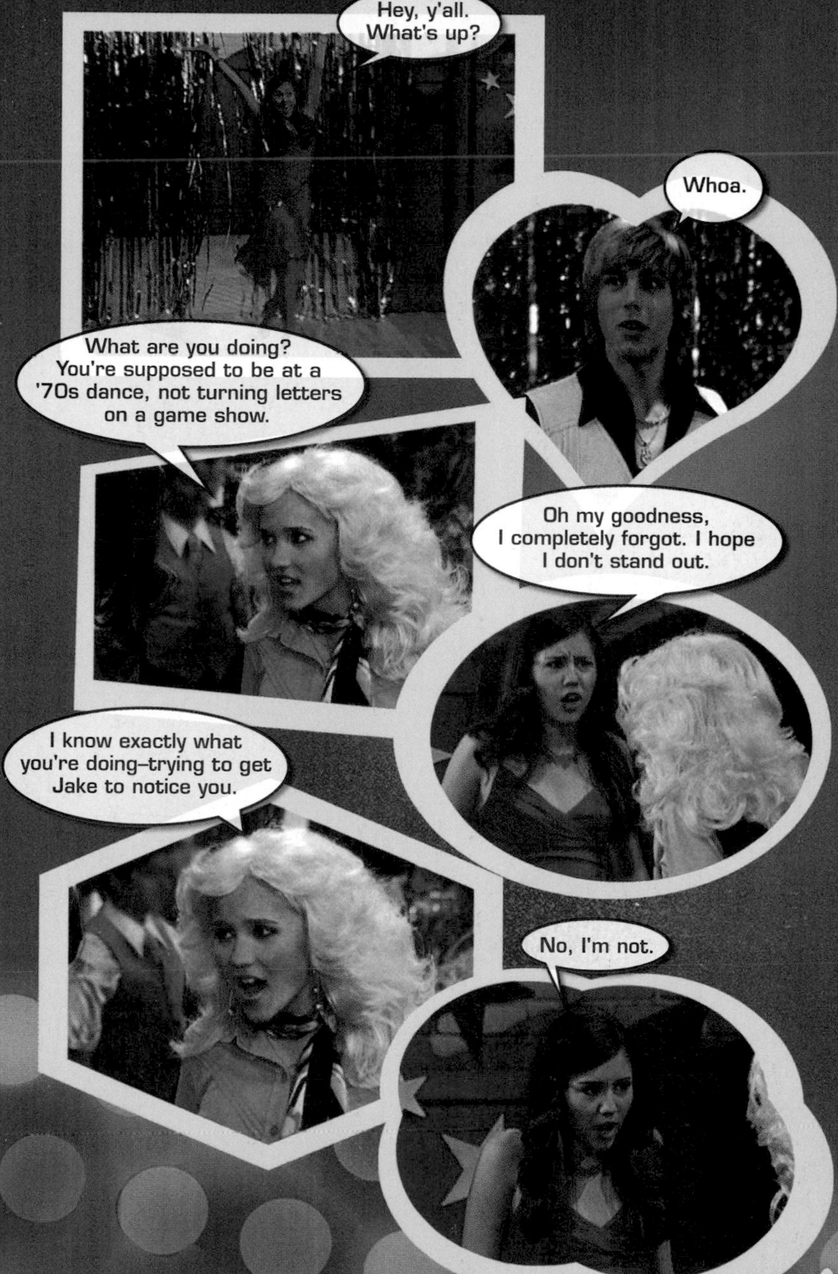
Hey, y'all. What's up?
Whoa.
What are you doing? You're supposed to be at a '70s dance, not turning letters on a game show.
Oh my goodness, I completely forgot. I hope I don't stand out.
I know exactly what you're doing–trying to get Jake to notice you.
No, I'm not.

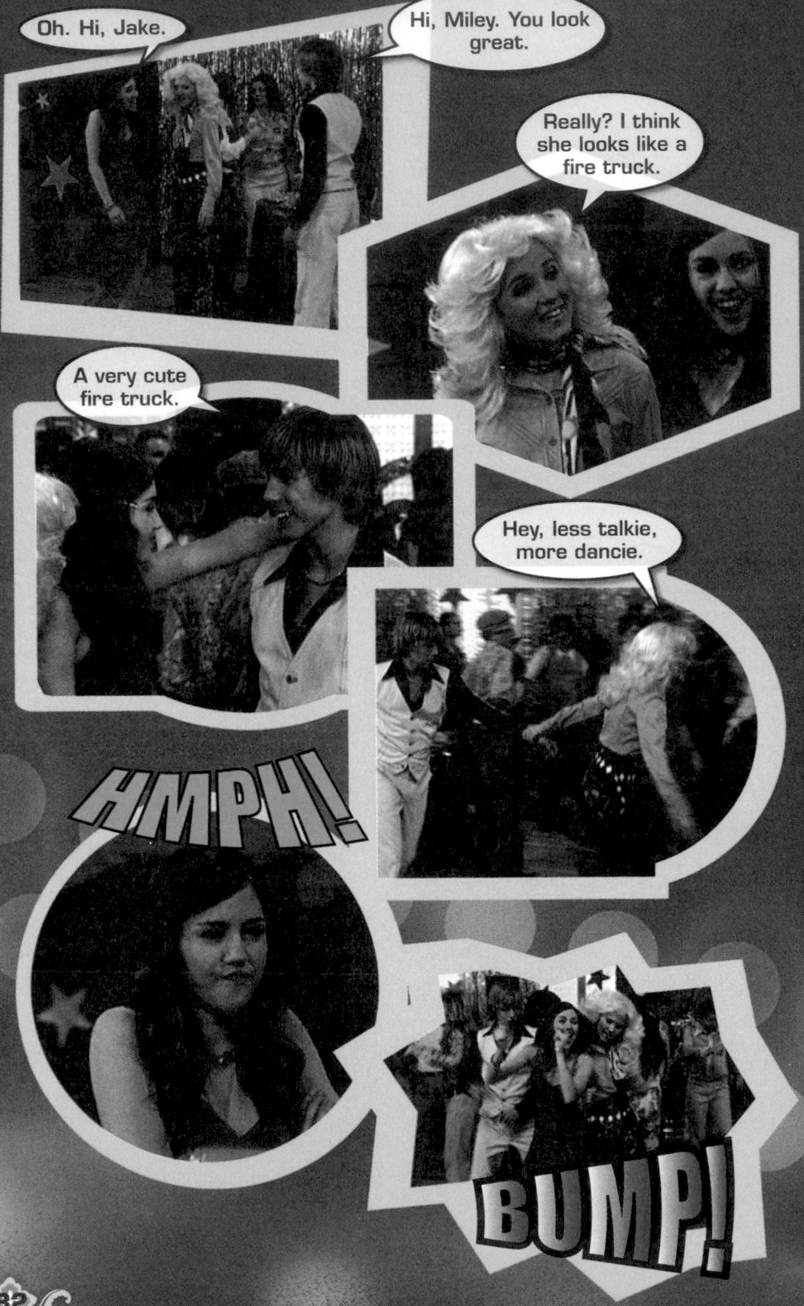
Oh. Hi, Jake.
Hi, Miley. You look great.
Really? I think she looks like a fire truck.
A very cute fire truck.
Hey, less talkie, more dancie.
HMPH!
BUMP!

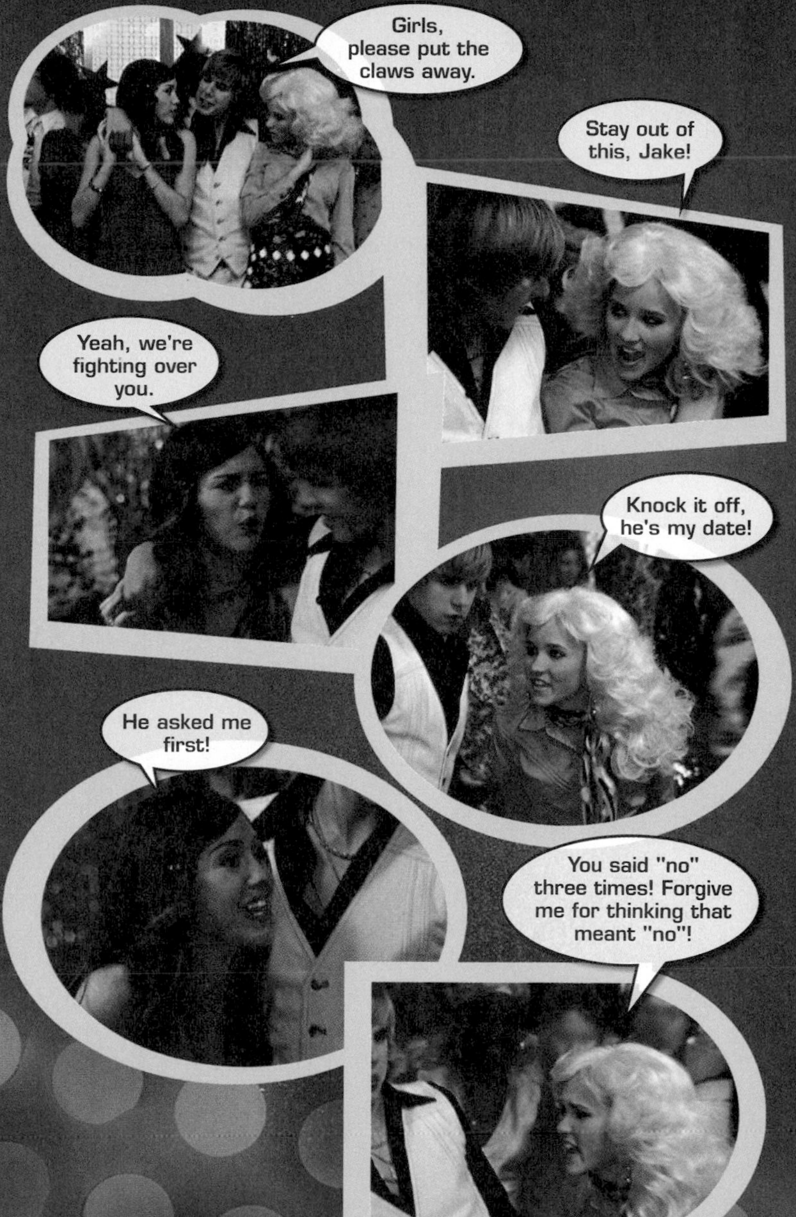
Girls, please put the claws away.
Stay out of this, Jake!
Yeah, we're fighting over you.
Knock it off, he's my date!
He asked me first!
You said "no" three times! Forgive me for thinking that meant "no"!

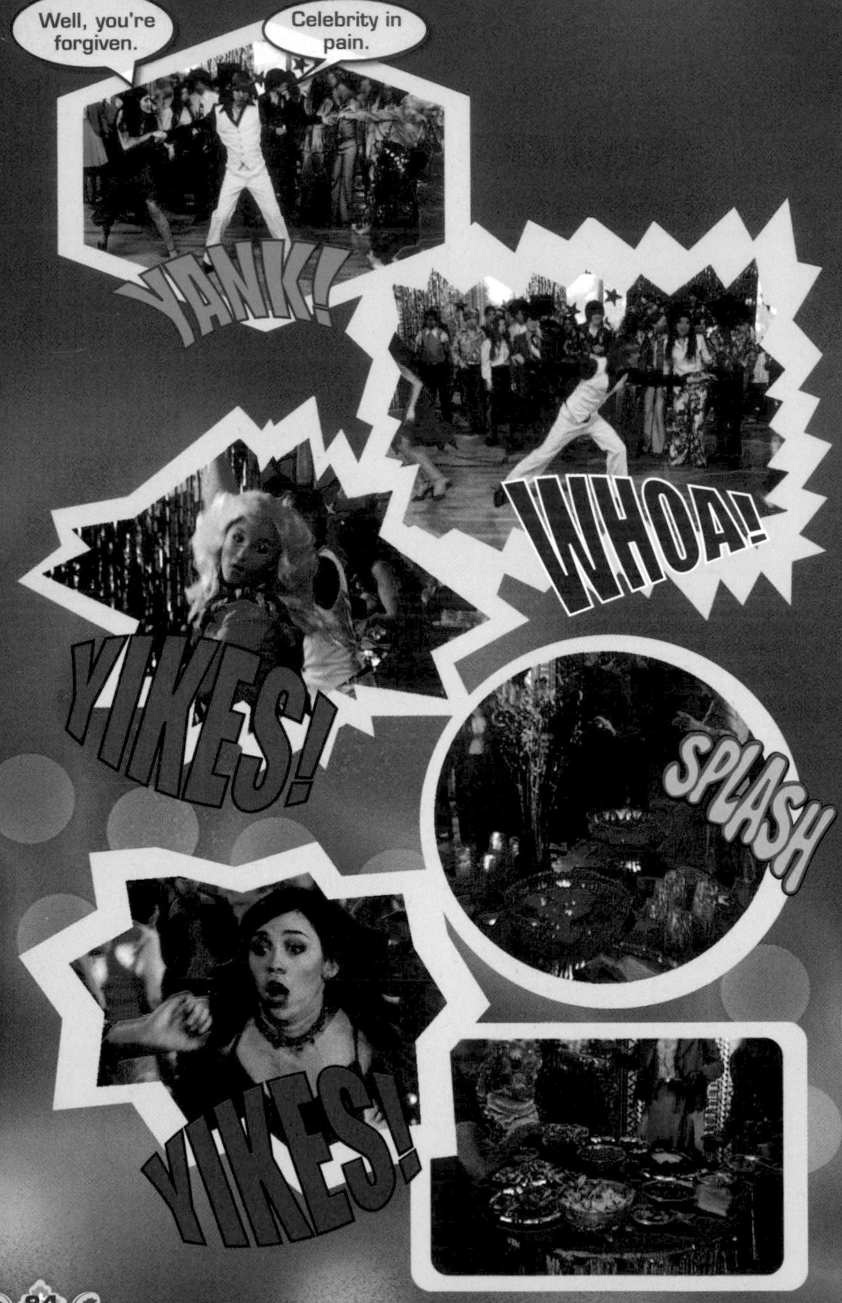
Well, you're forgiven.
Celebrity in pain.
YANK!
WHOA!
YIKES!
SPLASH
YIKES!

Congratulations. You made me look ridiculous in front of Jake.
Well, look what you did to me.
Hey, I'm not the one who tried to steal someone else's date. How could you do that to me?
...I don't know! It was just Jake and...he's just so cute...
...and that Thunder Mint...wow. And I kissed a dog. I think I deserve it!
Well, you can have him. I don't like him that much anyway.

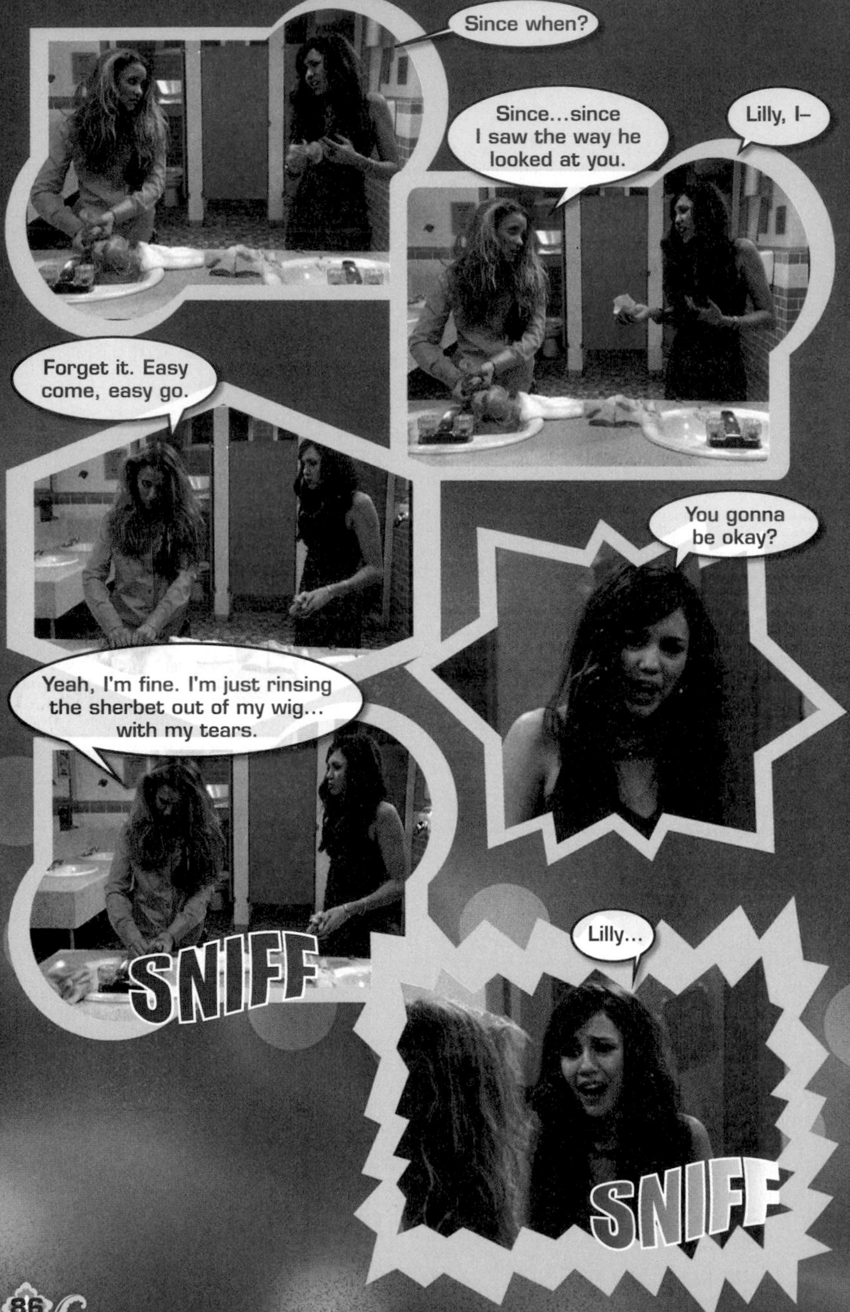
Since when?
Since...since I saw the way he looked at you.
Lilly, I–
Forget it. Easy come, easy go.
You gonna be okay?
Yeah, I'm fine. I'm just rinsing the sherbet out of my wig... with my tears.
SNIFF
Lilly...
SNIFF

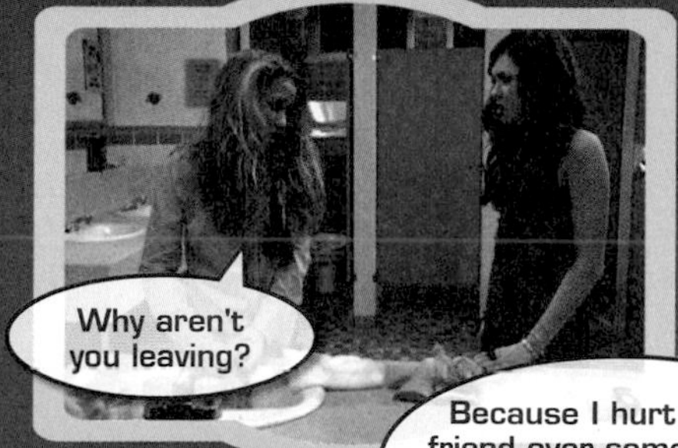
Why aren't you leaving?

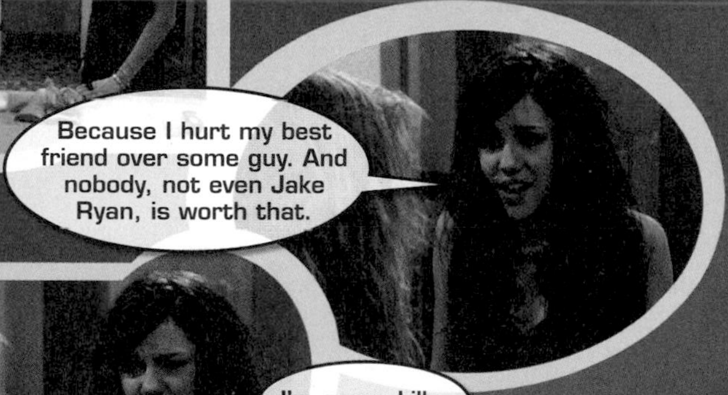
Because I hurt my best friend over some guy. And nobody, not even Jake Ryan, is worth that.

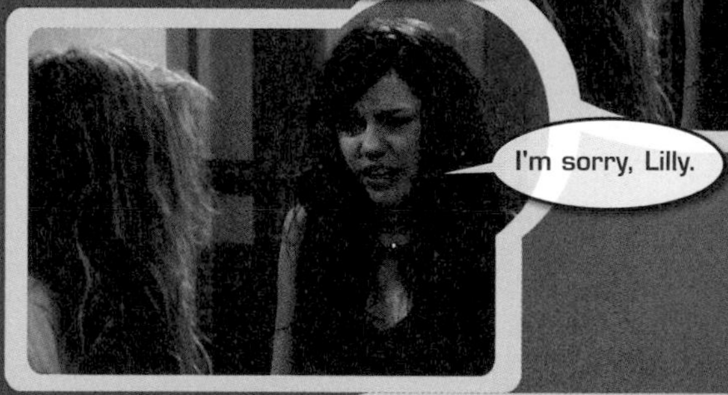
I'm sorry, Lilly.

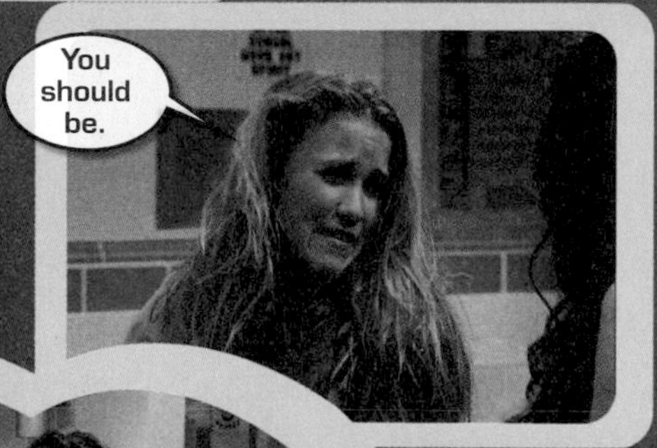
You should be.

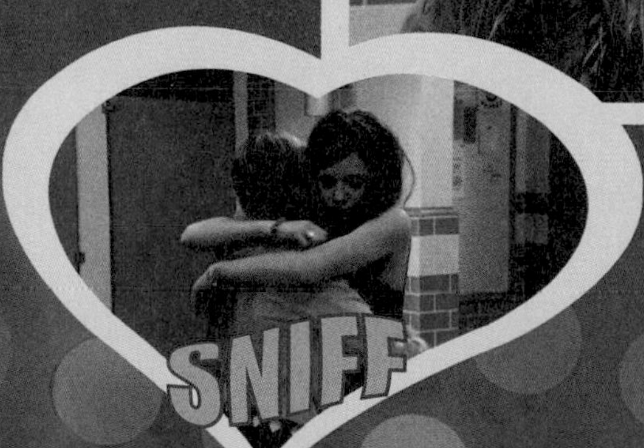
SNIFF

soon...

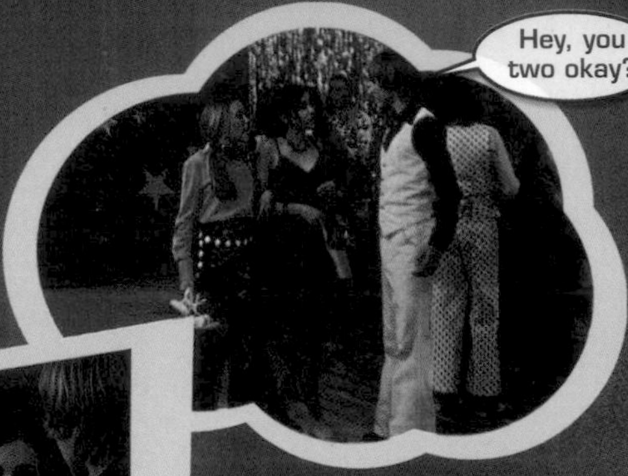
Hey, you two okay?

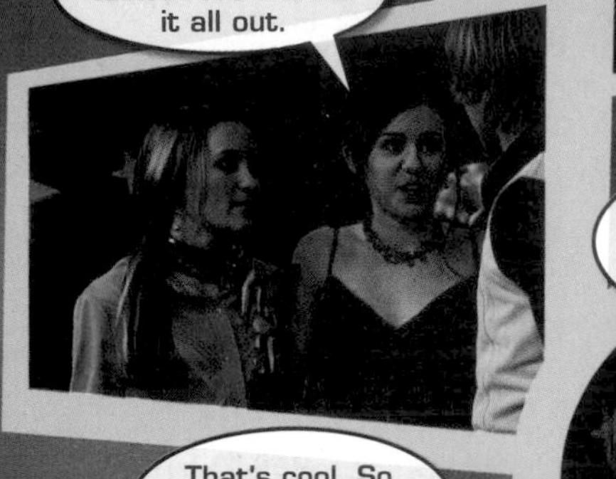
Yeah, we talked. We worked it all out.

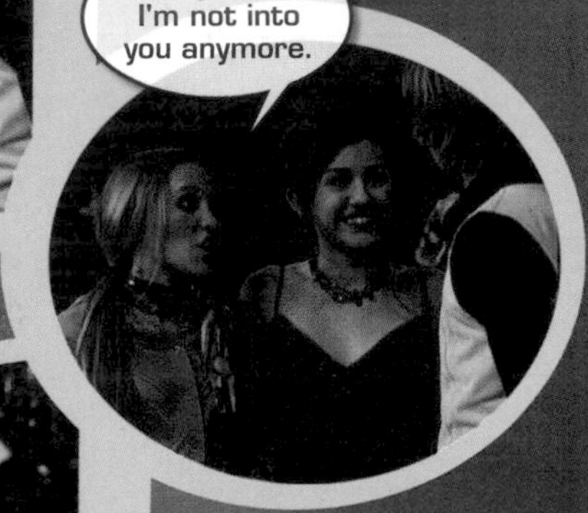
Sorry, Jake. I'm not into you anymore.

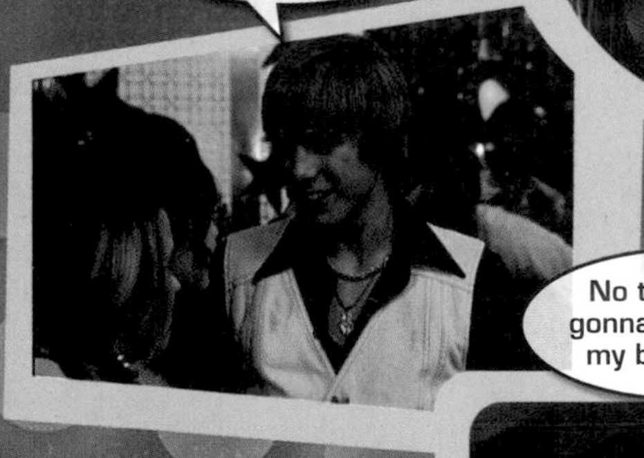
That's cool. So, Miley, you wanna dance?

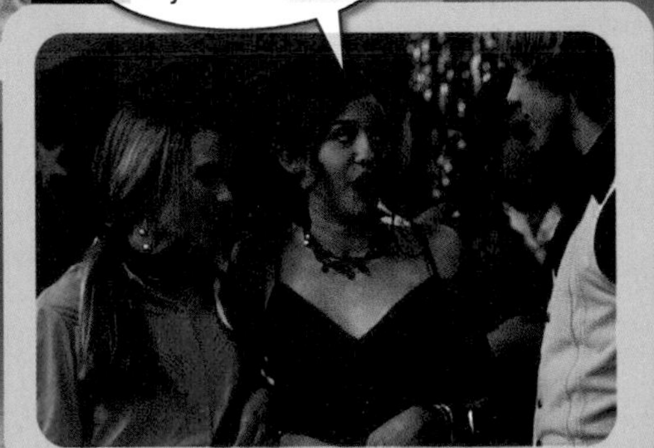
No thanks, I'm gonna dance with my best friend.

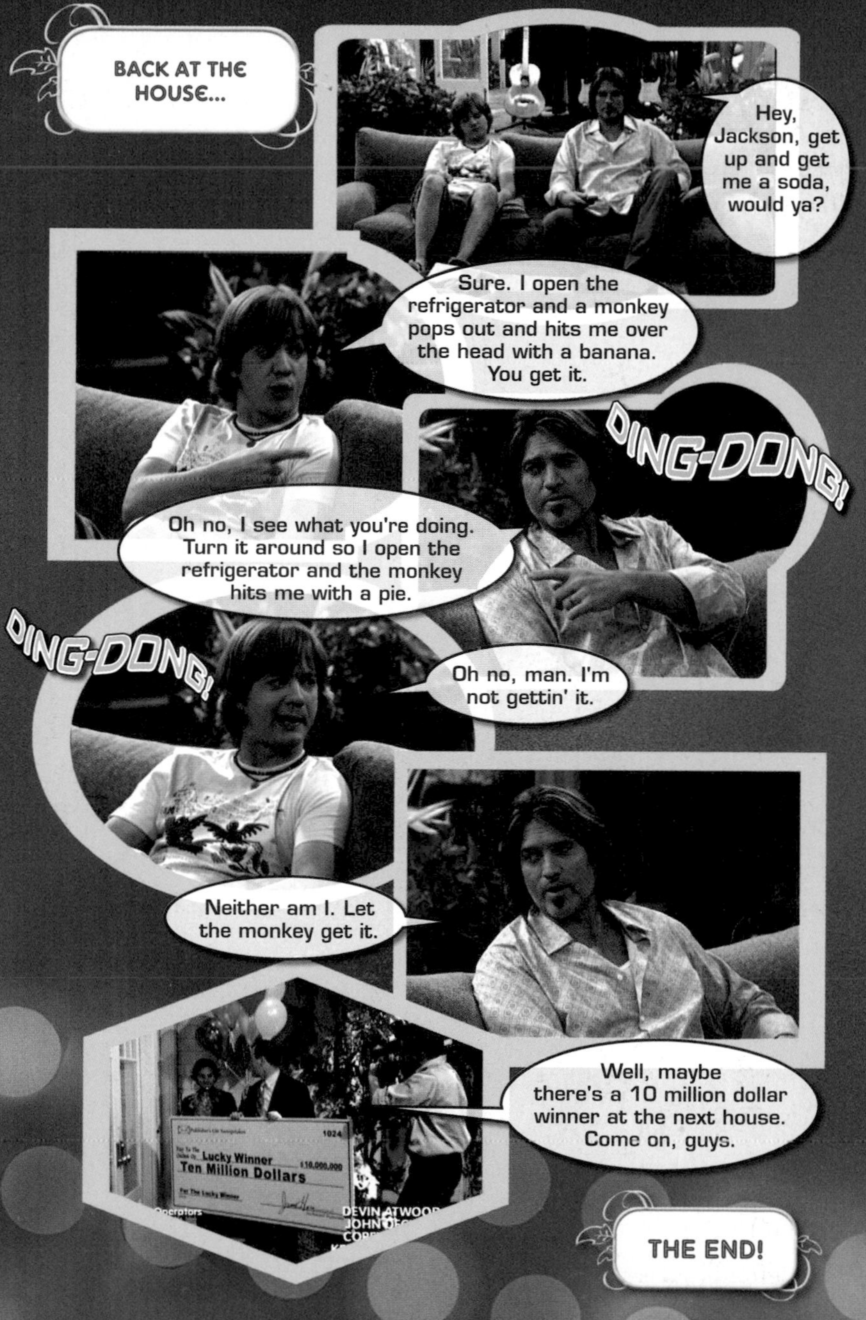
BACK AT THE HOUSE...
Hey, Jackson, get up and get me a soda, would ya?
Sure. I open the refrigerator and a monkey pops out and hits me over the head with a banana. You get it.
DING-DONG!
Oh no, I see what you're doing. Turn it around so I open the refrigerator and the monkey hits me with a pie.
DING-DONG!
Oh no, man. I'm not gettin' it.
Neither am I. Let the monkey get it.
1024
Lucky Winner
$10,000,000
Ten Million Dollars
Well, maybe there's a 10 million dollar winner at the next house. Come on, guys.
THE END!

Experience your favorite movies and TV shows in the palm of your hand...
TOKYOPOP
Disney presents a PIXAR film
THE INCREDIBLES
©2007 Disney Enterprises, Inc. Pixar Animation Studios. All Rights Reserved.
TOKYOPOP
Walt Disney Pictures presents
CHICKEN LITTLE
CINE-MANGA
The sky is falling!
©2007 Disney Enterprises, Inc.
Walt Disney's Cinderella
...with TOKYOPOP® CINE-MANGA® books!
©2007 Disney Enterprises, Inc.

- Aladdin
- Bambi
- Cars
- Chicken Little
- Cinderella
- Cinderella III
- Finding Nemo
- Hannah Montana
- High School Musical

- The Incredibles
- Kim Possible
- Lilo & Stitch: The Series
- Lizzie McGuire
- Pirates of the Caribbean: Dead Man's Chest
- Pooh's Heffalump Movie
- The Princess Diaries 2
- That's So Raven
- The Suite Life of Zack and Cody

## COLLECT THEM ALL!

Now available
wherever books are sold or at
www.TOKYOPOP.com/shop

DISNEP
HIGH SCHOOL MUSICAL

CINE-MANGA

DISNEP
The Suite Life
of Zack & Cody

TOKYOPOP

CINE-MANGA

TOKYOPOP
DISNEY
HANNAH MONTANA
CINE-MANGA
DISNEY
HANNAH MONTANA
TOKYOPOP
CINE-MANGA
SECRETS AND SUPERSNEAKS
AVAILABLE NOW AT TOKYOPOP!
© Disney Enterprises, Inc.

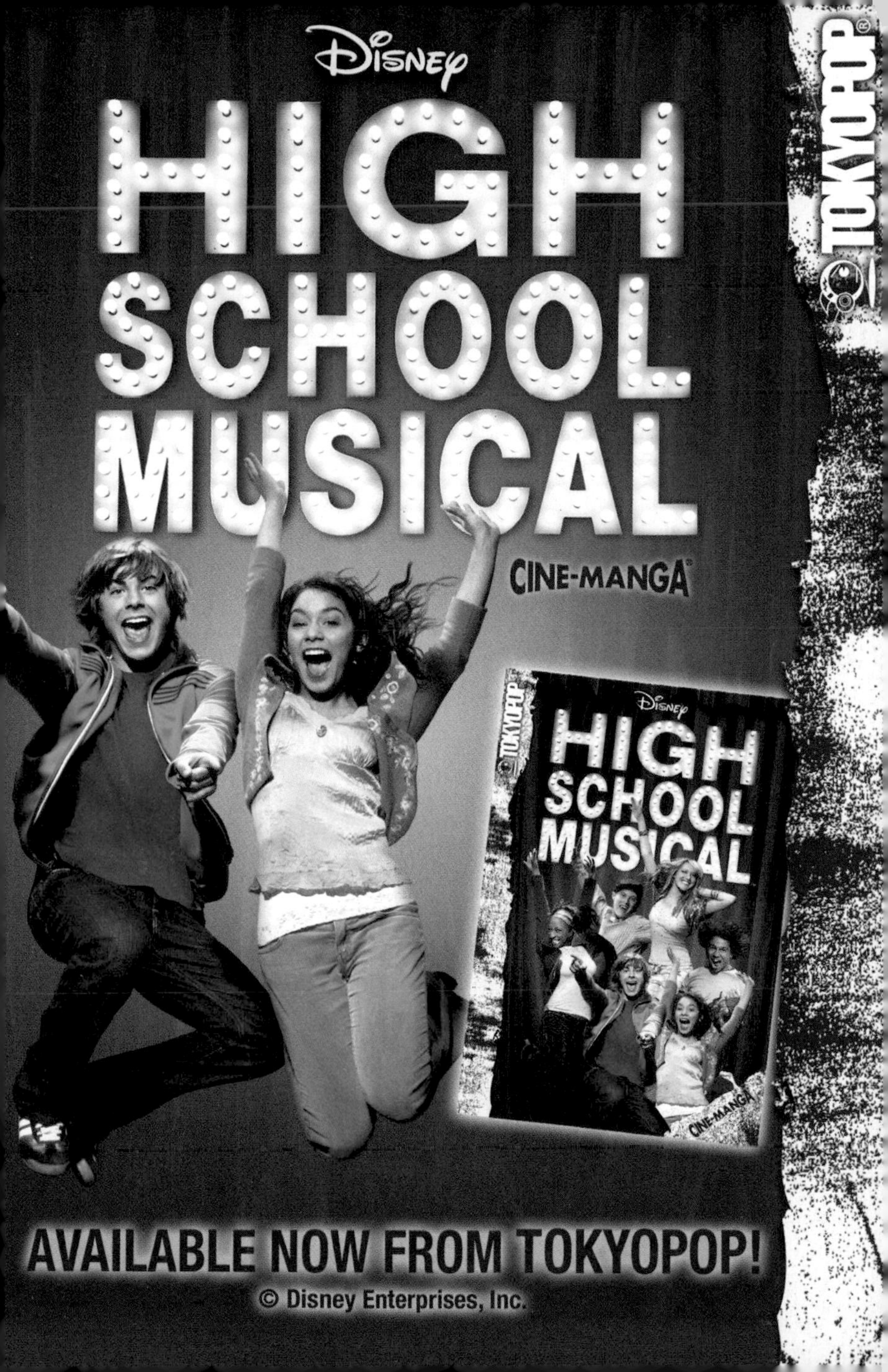

DISNEY
HIGH SCHOOL MUSICAL
CINE-MANGA
TOKYOPOP
AVAILABLE NOW FROM TOKYOPOP!
© Disney Enterprises, Inc.

# LiZZiE
## McGUiRE
### CINE-MANGA

**EVERYONE'S FAVORITE TEENAGER NOW HAS HER OWN CINE-MANGA®!**

TOKYOPOP

# that's SO raven

**TOKYOPOP**

# The future is now!

The hit show from Disney is
now a hot new Cine-Manga®!

**A** ALL AGES

**www.TOKYOPOP.com**

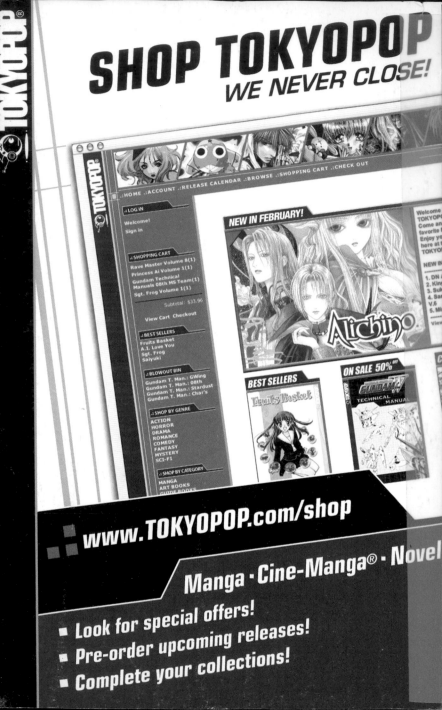